Between a Loch and a Hard Place

*Life, History, Climbing &
Mountain Rescue in Glencoe*

Davy Gunn

First published in 2024
By Davy Gunn

Copyright © 2024 Davy Gunn

Davy Gunn has asserted his right to
be identified as the author of this work.

Cover: Loch Leven and the Bidean Mountain Range.
(Photo by Davy Gunn.)

Printed by Imprint Digital, UK

Book production by Lumphanan Press
www.lumphananpress.co.uk

ISBN: 978-1-3999-9590-0

Contents

5	About the Author
7	Introduction
11	Geography, History and a Journey Down the Glen
19	Massacres and Jacobites
23	Lord Strathcona
25	The River Coe
29	The Gunn Family
36	Wanders with a Fishing Rod
40	Secondary School and Work
49	Mountaineering Adventures
57	A Guide's Tale
62	Fiona
65	Glencoe Classic Climbs
91	Mountain Accidents
97	Hamish and Mountain Rescue
102	Early Rescues
117	Mountain Medicine
127	Some Mountain Rescue Tales
158	Skiing
166	Avalanches and Head Games
176	The Psychological Cost of Mountain Accidents
183	Leaving Mountain Rescue
186	"Davy the Bike"
191	Loss and Finding My Way

About the Author

The author was born in Oban and brought up in the village of Carnoch, better known as Glencoe village. A Highland upbringing rich in community. Glencoe is an area steeped in bloody history, surrounded by mountains and cut through by the River Coe. Known for its infamous 1692 massacre, Glencoe is also famed for its mountaineering, with people coming from all over the world to climb its majestic peaks and test themselves on its rock and ice climbs. Glencoe Mountain Rescue Team has a long history of saving lives and of rescue from the West Highlands and has had a few of Scotland's best mountaineers as members. Not least was one of the rescue team founders, Hamish MacInnes.

This book gives some local history and insight into how a Highland boy lived beside a river that gave quietude and wonder as its silver leapers, the Atlantic salmon, forged up through its foamy waters into the mountains. And where the boy was to meet mountain folk who opened his eyes to a broader world and possibilities. This book is about a place. It could include other travels and experiences, but it doesn't as it's about my upbringing, and the community of Glencoe that formed the me that I wish to write about. The reader may find the climbing and rescue tales a bit technical using the terms and technicalities of the sport. The same is true for skiing. Forgive me as it's hard to convey some of these ascents and descents without these technical details. Skip past bits if necessary and just enjoy the book as a collection of impressions and tales.

Introduction

The River Coe journeys from mountain top to sea, clear and fast flowing. Its strath and its geography intertwined with my life as a journey to find myself. This book contains some tales of a life lived in this landscape and community. I have travelled a fair bit, climbed some bigger mountains, and been to some exotic places, but Glencoe is home, where I belong, not just where I come from. It is about some of the story of my life in Glencoe that I wanted to write.

Neil Gunn, the famous Scottish author, wrote a book, *Highland River*, which has Kenn, the main character, questing life's meaning, following migrating salmon to the source of the river. Young and old, Kenn and I were on a similar quest. The source for Kenn was on high Caithness moorland, for me the rugged Glencoe peaks and ridges. Finding the source of the river Coe, high in the lofty Argyll peaks, the trickles, rivulets, streams tumbling steeply westward to Lochs Leven, Linnhe and the ocean. My life journey has been betwixt these mountains from sea to summit. Between a loch and a hard place of austere Dalriadan rock and the Andesite of the Bidean mountain range. The salmon, a symbol of Celtic wisdom migrating up these fast-flowing streams, has given me just a glimpse of the hazelnut of knowledge, and for that I am grateful.

Putting finger to keyboard to write required some consideration of what my story really is. I concluded that it is just the tale of a pretty average Highland boy, fortuitous to have been loved and brought up in a close community. Not a tale of hardship, perhaps only a journey of self-discovery, finding meaning in life and an awakening to how lucky he has been to have worked with and met so many great characters. These are stories that eulogise some important people, and in other places just some tales. I hope it entertains and maybe informs a little.

This story is dedicated to my family. My mother and father for the many sleepless nights while I was wandering the hills, and especially for the stress when they saw our lights not moving late one night cragfast high up on Aonach Dubh. Fiona for her support, patience, love, forbearance and friendship over the years. She was truly a partner on and off the rope. My children, Esther, Duncan and Rebekah, must often have wondered if Dad might come back from a night on the hill rescuing. I hope I made it up to them. They are clever, having inherited their mother's brains, looks and love of gardening and my love of the hills and wild places. I love them dearly.

A very special thanks must go to Lucy Morrice, a good writer, who helped guide a poor writer with terrible spelling. She has done her very best to help poor text become more readable. This book is no great literary work and that's all down to me. It is a lot better than it would have been without her patience and support.

The river is the thread
Running stitches through time
Gathering mountains, forests and sea
And binding me to this land

– **Lucy Morrice**

Geography, History and a Journey Down the Glen

For most visitors, Glencoe starts at the Blackmount, passing Bridge of Orchy after ascending the sinuous bends of the A82 up to a high point, then crossing onto the moor of Rannoch with its small lochs and vistas across what may appear a barren, lifeless landscape, although in reality it is anything but lifeless. Perhaps not the life and fertility the wood had as part of the great wood of Caledon, but still home to Arctic char, perch and genetically unique brown trout, sometimes with three distinct genetic populations of trout in one loch such as Loch Laidon. Otters, red deer, osprey, golden and sea eagles, pine marten and a host of wildfowl abound.

Passing over the moor, Glencoe ski mountain appears on your left and Kingshouse Hotel on your right. Jumping out of the landscape at you on the left is Buachaille Etive Mòr, translated as the Great Herdsman of Etive. For locals arriving at the junction of Glencoe and Glen Etive, this is the real beginning of Glencoe. Seeing the Buachaille while crossing the moor is always a heart-warming feeling if you have been away for a while, and it never ceases to impress. Below the Buachaille is a small dark climber's hut named "Jacksonville" after a member of the Creag Dubh mountaineering club, Jimmy Jackson. Altnafeadh and the climbing cottage of Lagangarbh come up next. From Altnafeadh a path known as "The Devil's Staircase" crosses over to Kinlochleven and Blackwater Dam as part of the West Highland Way. This path was given its name from a tale from the old Kingshouse Hotel, where, when playing cards with a stranger, a player looked under the table and saw the stranger had cloven feet. A similar tale is told at the other Kingshouse Hotel in Balquhidder where a cattle drover also played cards with Auld Nick. Archive material of the renowned folklorist and ethnologist Calum Maclean (1915–1960) shows tales involving the Devil and card games like this occurred elsewhere in the Highlands. Perhaps as a warning against gambling! The Devil's Staircase path also gained a notorious reputation during the building of the Blackwater hydroelectric dam, as Irish navvies would travel over the hill to Kingshouse for refreshments and, in winter conditions, not always survive the return journey. The tale of the Blackwater Dam construction is immortalised in the book *Children of the Dead End* by Patrick MacGill. Still in print, it's well worth reading.

Up and over the next high point in the A82, the famous "Three Sisters" come into view, the road now descending past the narrow gorge and its waterfall on the left, down past Allt na Ruigh on the right with the Aonach Eagach Ridge, a famous notched mountaineering expedition, above. Scrambling along the Aonach Eagach for its three-mile length is not for the faint hearted. On the left of the A82, valleys seam their way up into the Bidean nan Bian Range. The most walked of the deep cut valleys is Allt Coire Gabhail, better known as "The Lost Valley", a secluded valley where the cattle-raiding

MacDonald clan were reputed to hide their spoils. Things flatten out as you pass Loch Achtriochtan, with Ossian's Cave on Aonach Dubh on its north face above, and the cottage of Achnambeithach nestled up against the foot of its west face above the Lochan. You are now in the Strath of Glencoe and at a road junction where you may either drive straight down the main A82 passing the National Trust for Scotland visitor centre, perhaps calling in for a nice coffee and information on the Glen, its geology, flora and fauna, mountain history, the massacre at the interpretation centre, or take a right onto "the old road" and pass the site of the infamous MacDonald massacre near Clachaig Hotel, a famous mountaineering pub. The Red Squirrel campsite below this pub is a convenient location for parking up overnight or staying at the Scottish or Independent youth hostels further down. There is a walking and cycle track next to the old road. It passes a rock known locally as the Devil's Fingers where Auld Nick lifted a rock to escape the underworld and, pulling himself up, burned four perfect finger slots into the small cliff at the side. Travel downwards over the old humpback bridge, over the river Coe, and you are in the village.

With its stunning and dramatic landscape, the area has been a popular filming location for various movies. Films have been made in Glencoe since celluloid was invented. Seeing the "Three Sisters" and "Buachaille Etive Mòr" as a backdrop to films or advertisements is a common thing. Locals were often hosts to actors or became extras in bigger productions. Possibly the first really big film was Walt Disney's production of Robert Louis Stevenson's book *Kidnapped* starring Peter Finch as Alan Breck Stewart and James MacArthur as

David Balfour. The salmon ladder, the "Three Sisters" and Alan Breck's rock next to the A82 road below An t-Sron are recognisable in the film. Several climbing films were also made, and in 1969 a BBC live outside broadcast of climbers took place on the west face of Aonach Dubh's "E" Buttress, climbing three of its classic routes. Pre-digital, this was a huge undertaking with thick power cables running up to the cliffs. A film of the Glencoe Massacre by Austin Campbell was made in 1972 with James Robertson Justice in the lead as MacIain.

The BBC climbing films all involved Hamish MacInnes as both a safety advisor and, as Hamish had already been making climbing films of his own, as a cameraman. Films such as *The Eiger Sanction* and *Five Days One Summer* had Hamish as safety advisor. Later he made his own films such as *Eagle's Eye View of Glencoe*, which had Fiona, my wife, and Jane Naismith climbing a route on the north face of Gearr Aonach. In 1991 *Palin's Progress* was filmed with Michael Palin of Monty Python fame and Ang Pherba, a sherpa, traversing the Aonach Eagach Ridge.

Monty Python and the Holy Grail was filmed in the area using the Lost Valley gorge for the Bridge of Death and Stalker Castle, Appin as Castle Aaargh. Hagrid's hut and the Hogwarts covered bridge from *Harry Potter and the Prisoner of Azkaban* highlights Glencoe's connection to the magic world of J.K. Rowling's series of books. The iconic scene with Daniel Craig as James Bond and Judie Dench as "M" in the film *Skyfall* in Glen Etive further emphasises the cinematic appeal of Glencoe and the surrounding area. The film *Rob Roy*, featuring Liam Neeson, used the location extensively to bring the story of the Scottish folk hero to life. The more recent films *Outlaw King*, starring Chris Pine as Robert the Bruce, and *Mary Queen of Scots*, with Saoirse Ronan in the lead, showcase Glencoe's versatility as a backdrop for historical dramas.

Classic films like *Highlander* employed many locals in set creation or as extras. Most of us will not forget the final battle scene. Extras went on strike for more money as it was cold, wet and windy. More money and seven cases of whisky did the trick. A tour bus of pensioners didn't get the joke when 200 drunken Highlanders with swords charged the bus for a bit of fun.

Local man Peter Weir and I temporarily moved a cairn for a scene in the *Highlander* film. The cairn where (apparently) Queen Victoria sat with John Brown and had a picnic, and where Wordsworth looked back on leaving the Glen, claiming "nothing here but Highland pride and hunger". On moving the cairn, we found a small wooden ciste under it. We did not wish to desecrate anything, but our noses got the better of us, so we easily prised open the box to find a wee wax bag which, as it turned out, held a desiccated turd. It could well have been the Queen's, but we will never know. Further investigation of the box revealed it to be lined with newspaper. Just visible was *The Sunday Post*, dated 1953. We reverentially re-interred the sacred turd, and after the film shot was taken, which was a blacksmith's forge scene, we carefully rebuilt the cairn in its original position with the turd at its centre. There this piece of history remains. This area is now known as Ralston's Cairn, but it's got nothing to do with "Ralston", whose memorial cross is above near the climbing hut known as the Drey.

I did some medical cover on the film *Rob Roy* and, as is common working on films, it was long days of boredom with thankfully great food from the chuck wagons. Far more fun are the shorter films, like adverts. Local man David Cooper and I worked on one for a new Peugeot car many years ago. We had to dress up as toffs and scramble about with a stuntman in the waterfall below the well-known viewpoint at the gorge. Rescue team members also enjoyed a lot of film work on outside broadcasts such as one over a month in preparation on Ben Nevis in winter, which sadly couldn't go out live due to the weather. Helicoptering about the Ben for a month in the better weather beforehand and with a good daily wage was very nice. The scenic beauty of Glencoe will continue to attract filmmakers, making it a prominent location in the world of cinema in years to come, I am sure.

Upper and Lower Carnoch, more commonly known as the village of Glencoe, nestles at the foot of the Strath of the Glen next to Loch Leven. The area is rich in history. Pre-Christian neolithic at Onich to the north and the standing stone at Clach-a-Charra. At North Ballachulish, the Ballachulish Goddess (now in the National Museum of Scotland) from 600 BCE. Later came Fingal, a great Celtic hero and leader of the Feinn warriors of Gaelic mythology. Glencoe was his legendary home, and his memory is preserved in a number of place names. For example, Sgor nam Fiannaidh and Ossian's Cave on Aonach Dubh. The cave of Ossian was made famous by James Macpherson in his tales and epic heroic poems. Made up the poems may have been, but they are beautifully written. There are some defensive trenches on the Pap of Glencoe where the Fionn warriors defended against Viking raiders at a battle between Fionn mac Cumhaill and a raiding party of 40 longships which sailed up the narrows past Ballachulish into Loch Leven. They were defeated and their chief, Earragan, was apparently killed by a Goll MacMorna. The Dewar manuscripts, a collection of local oral history, has a detailed account of this raiding party and the battle. While the poems of Ossian are mythical, there is evidence that the Fionn really were here, as the place names support it.

Obvious on Loch Leven are a group of small islands, one of which is known locally as the Burial Island because of its graves, but Eilean Munde is the proper name. The island was named after St Fintan Mundus of Argyle, an Irish rival of St Columba. Mundus came from Iona in the seventh century and established several churches, including the one on the Burial Island, now in ruins. Legend has it that Columba and Mundus were in close competition to be first to land on the Island of Lismore to set up a Christian community. Rowing to shore, Columba was ahead of Mundus. So Mundus cut off his finger and threw it past Columba onto the shore, thus claiming the island.

Mundus was of the Ui-Neill clan in Ireland and trained as a monk. He arrived in Alba (Scotland) in about AD 600 and founded several churches. His final one was Eilean Munde. The church burned down in approximately 1495 and was rebuilt. The last service was in July of 1693, which is just one year after the infamous massacre. The island is the burial place of both local Clan MacDonald and Clan MacInnes, each having separate landing sites on the island. It was said that the island was haunted by the spirit of the last person buried there, who could not enter Paradise until the next was buried.

Over the centuries the MacDougalls of Lorn managed to build up an empire in western Scotland. However, this collapsed in 1308 when they sided in favour of Balliol against Robert the Bruce. In thanks for his support during the conflict, Robert the Bruce gifted Glencoe to Angus Og, the chief of the MacDonalds. Angus Og left Glencoe to his son Iain Fraoch, who founded the Clan MacIain Abrach of Glencoe, who were to be the famous/infamous MacIain/MacDonalds of Glencoe, later hounded and massacred.

Massacres and Jacobites

The cause of the Massacre stemmed from a feud between MacDonalds and Argyll Campbells. The Glencoe MacDonalds raided and thieved cattle, often from Campbell land. This rumbled on into the middle of the 17th century and Scotland's involvement in the Scottish Wars of the Covenant, in which the MacDonalds and the Campbells were on different sides. The MacDonalds were associated with the Royalist and rebel cause and the Campbells increasingly with the government. It was, in some ways, a fight between the diverse ways of life of lawless Highlanders and centralised government.

On 27th August 1692, King William III in London offered a pardon to all the clans who had fought against him or raided their neighbours, such as MacDonalds into Campbell lands. However, they had to take an oath of allegiance before a magistrate by 1st January 1692. Not complying meant death. Clan Chief MacIain of Glencoe, somewhat reluctantly it seems, agreed to take the oath. He went to Inverlochy in Fort William, where the commanding officer John Hill told him that he could not receive his oath of allegiance. He must travel to Inveraray. Inveraray is a long journey in winter by pony from Glencoe, let alone after going to Fort William over the high passes. MacIain finally reached Inveraray on January

6th, well after the deadline. MacIain believed that, despite his delay in taking the oath, he and his clan were now safe. He would not have known that troops had already been assembled at Inveraray and given orders to exterminate the whole clan. The force left for Glencoe on 1st February, commanded by Captain Robert Campbell of Glen Lyon, a man with a grudge against the Glencoe MacDonalds. Captain Campbell asked for quarters for his 130 soldiers, and unaware of what was planned, the MacDonalds billeted them for ten days.

The night of the 12th of February 1692, Campbell received an order to kill all MacDonalds under 70 years of age, starting at 5am the next morning. In the early hours of a wintry morning, they set about the massacre of their hosts, who they had been living with. It was an act of treachery when hospitality had been given. Thirty-seven at least were killed. Some escaped to the hills, only to die in the harsh winter conditions. With orders from King William and the Secretary for State of Scotland, approved by the Scottish Privy Council and planned and carried out by elements of the Scots army, the Massacre of Glencoe was not a clan feud. It was genocide.

During the Jacobite risings, and in particular the 1745 Rebellion, the surrounding area of North Argyll and Lochaber was very much out for the Jacobite cause. The Stewarts of Appin in particular came out for the Prince and suffered vicious punishments after Culloden with land forfeiture, burnings and retribution.

Charles Stewart of Ardsheal, a Jacobite commander, spent some time hiding in the hills and then fled to France, dying at Sens in France on the 15th of March 1757, having escaped in 1746. He had been sentenced to death in absentia and his estate had been confiscated by the government. The estate was returned to the family in 1788. There are many Ardsheal caves dotted around the hillsides to the south of Glencoe where Ardsheal hid when being hunted. The infamous Appin murder, where an innocent man was hanged as an example, was a direct Campbell and government message that no more Jacobitism would be tolerated, even if it were to cost James Stewart his life. His only crime was being Appin Stewart heir apparent, and not hiding his views of the government factor for forfeited estates, Colin Campbell of Glenure. At the local ale house at Acharn in Duror, he was heard to air views against the factor. James Stewart was hanged on 8th November 1752 at a specially erected scaffold. His final utterance, "False witnesses rose; to my charge things I not knew they laid. They, to the spoiling of my soul, me ill for good repaid" from Psalm 35.

His corpse was left hanging on a gibbet above Ballachulish narrows for months, the bones wired up so it could hang for longer!

Between 1740 and 1767 a military road was built passing the east end of Glencoe, past Kinlochleven to Fort William, by Major William Caulfield, successor to General Wade. This road was for faster troop movement between garrisons to aid in the pacification of the Highland clans post the 1745 Jacobite Rebellion. In 1785 a road was built through the actual Pass of Glencoe. The years that followed the building of the road through the Glencoe Pass were relatively quiet historically.

Parcels of land were used to settle debts or rented out for grazing sheep. Land owned by Cameron of Lochiel or other landowners who by this time had managed to get their forfeited lands returned. Land that had been taken for being Jacobite sympathisers or fighting for the Jacobite cause. Many of them were at Culloden. By this time they had thrown themselves into the new United Kingdom, its growing empire and the prosperity that came from it. Ironically, at least to the author, some of these once fiercely independent clan leaders and ex-Jacobites got a taste for money, a posh accent, military glory for King, Queen and country, slave plantations and London clubs. MacIain's successors, however, were not among the ones who prospered in the new empire. Many MacDonalds escaped a subsistence economy, having emigrated, some marrying Native Americans across an ocean, making new lives in Nova Scotia or British Columbia, perhaps having mountains named after them such as MacDonald peak in the Canadian Rockies. Those left in Glencoe were subsistence crofters and farmers, and much later workers at the new aluminium factory in Kinlochleven, which started production in 1909. Many also became forest workers after the forming of the Forestry Commission in 1919. Their offspring also often moved to the cities for better opportunities or emigrated. It is not so different now, as the Highlands bleed out young talent, and what remains instead of rusty corrugated iron dereliction and bare stone walls of old croft houses are holiday homes, outrageous land values and an ageing population.

Lord Strathcona

Lord Strathcona or John Smith, as was his given name, had emigrated from Forres to work for the Hudson's Bay Company. He became a very wealthy man, famous for driving "the last spike" on the Canadian Pacific Railway and as a founder of modern Canada. On the 23rd of August 1897, he was created Baron Strathcona and Mount Royal of Glencoe in the Diamond Jubilee honours list of Queen Victoria. He apparently wanted to be Lord Glencoe but had to settle for Lord Strathcona. He created a large estate at the lower end of the Strath of Glencoe, and built a large house, which is now a private hotel above the village, next to what locals call the Lochan. The house became a World War I convalescent home and was gifted to Argyll Council in the 1940s. In the 1950s it became a maternity hospital. My sister Kathleen was born there. In 1970 it became a geriatric hospital. Seldom have an older generation seen out their sunset years in such opulence. The nearby Lochan and woodlands were built and planted to help Strathcona's wife Isabella feel less homesick for her native Canada. Part "Metis" (Native American) Isabella may not have ever been part of a licensed marriage to John Smith, although they had a bush wedding, and later a private ceremony at a trading post. As he became one of the wealthiest men on the planet, society turned a blind eye.

She hated Glencoe for being so wet, so they built another big house on the Island of Coll where the microclimate was more amenable. The rest of the time, London was the place to be. Strathcona was a philanthropic person and self-made. Although connected to Glencoe by his Barony, it is Canada where he is best known.

Ownership of the pass of Glencoe, including some parts of Strathcona's estate, passed through several hands until 1935. Largely due to Scottish mountaineer Percy Unna, who fronted the money, the Scottish National Trust was able to buy a part of the Glencoe estate, including the Bidean mountain range. The big house belonged to Argyll County Council then later Highland Regional Council. The river was kept by the Kitson/Black descendants of Strathcona, and the Lochan and forest bought by the Forestry Commission. Some of the Strathcona estate, including a section of the River Coe, was bought by a descendant of MacIain, local man Alister MacDonald, via donations given by MacDonalds from all over the world and a generous family donation. It is looked after by Glencoe Heritage Trust, a registered SCIO (Scottish Charitable Incorporated Organisation) created to preserve and keep the land in its undeveloped natural state. Glencoe and its village is now a year-round mountaineering and visitor destination. Sadly, Glencoe makes the news from tragedies on its mountains, of which I will write more later. And, more positively, from many movies and advertisements filmed in its unique landscape.

The River Coe

High on one of the Bidean range's finest tops, Stob Coire Sgreamhach, strong south-westerly winds blow. Cold, snow-laden wind full of moisture from its journey, polar cold mixing with maritime Atlantic moisture blown eastward until hitting the slopes of Glencoe. There it drops wet, thick and heavy snow, carried over the ridges to be dumped into the lee of Coire Eilde, forming Bidean's finest cornices along the southeast ridge overlooking the Lairig Eilde, which was once a coffin route for MacDonalds of Glen Etive and Glencoe. There the snow will stay freezing all winter until spring arrives and it slowly thaws its way down into the Allt Coir Eilde with its steep sides and a canyon at the foot. Above, on the ridgeline to Beinn Fhada, is "the bad step", an avoidable feature on a ridge once decorated by a rusty wire rope extending from the Coire Gabhail over the step and into Coire Eilde. A barrage balloon from Clydebank landed here in WWII. Escaped most likely from heavy German bombing, it had floated its way over, dragging its hawser, and come down on the Coire Gabhail flank of Beinn Fhada. Once discovered, its silk was gathered and coveted by climbers, who manufactured clothing from it.

The meltwater trickles into adjoining rivulets and forms streams cascading into the often foamy torrent of the Allt

Lairig Eilde down to the present-day A82 and the iconic waterfall where it is joined by streams off the Coire Meannarclach. Down it tumbles through gorges and over waterfalls until it meets with Allt Coire Gabhail and what was in the ancient past the river's course, the Allt Doire Bheith below Allt na Ruigh, and joins streams coming down from Am Bodach and Sron Garbh. "The Meeting of Three Waters" is now the River Coe and the first accessible place that even the hardiest of salmon could get to. Nutrient poor and stripped clear of anything that could sustain life, its crystal waters hide nothing. And yet lurking under stones and eddies, if you know where to look, are beautifully marked little brown trout that appear and disappear from who knows where. Downwards to Achtriochtan and the first pool in the river that once upon a time salmon could be seen, Polldubh Achtriochtan. Off it tumbles and braids into Loch Achtriochtan, the saviour of the last of the silver travellers, providing sanctuary and a nursery for both juvenile salmon and its lovely little brown trout, some of whom leave, genetically pre-programmed to be anadromous and so make the sea their home some of the time. These "sea trout" are amazing fish. Silver travellers who do not make the grand tour of the salmon, preferring not to travel more than ten miles at the most from their natal river, but growing fast from a better diet at sea than river, these once abundant fish are very exposed to the sea lice of salmon farms and have been almost wiped out in some locations.

Down from Achtriochtan the river gathers momentum and size. Soon the "Salmon Ladder" is reached. Before this fish pass was made, salmon were trapped there. In the 1920s the building of the salmon ladder opened the way up to the Loch.

Locals John Gillenvore and Davie, his brother, caught a 28lb salmon here in the 1920s, taking it home in a wheelbarrow.

Down past Torren and the Signal Rock, having passed through a deep gorge, the river reappears at the deep dark Achnacon pool. There is a Pacific Northwest feel here with big Douglas firs, silver spruce and the Torren lochs nestling under the Signal Rock. This rocky outcrop is where the signal for the Massacre allegedly was given, due to its prominence and visibility to both the lower and upper glen settlements where troops were billeted. Further downriver, past the Red Squirrel campsite, the river tumbles until it joins what is now Glencoe Heritage Trust land where the "Devil's Fingers" stream joins at the Dyke pool.

Downriver from here is Inverigan, where once there was a settlement, and where the river has braided out between the A82 and a retaining dyke on the other side. The dyke from Torren down was built to contain the river on its north side. The aptly named Greenpool is further downriver. A popular swimming spot for local kids and a once good fishing pool when salmon were running. The old Bridge of Coe is downstream, with its dark pool below where once we could lean over a rock and see silver salmon safely hiding deep below under a ledge. The salmon were resting, having ascended the formidable waterfall further downstream after coming up through the tidal pool fresh off the tide. The falls and tidal pool have holes, caves and smooth rock from aeons of water erosion. This pool up to the falls was at one time the best fishing spot when the river was in flood but is now more popular as a swimming spot. At one time hundreds of salmon and sea trout would pass through here. Sadly they are mostly gone. The river Coe has been good to me. It has kept me sane during times of poor mental health and been a source of solace from grief. It is a place of good memories. It is also where I met my wife of 44 years for the first time. It is a special place.

The Gunn Family

My father Angus (Angie) Gunn was born at Kinloch Teacuis in Morvern, where his father was a schoolteacher and crofter. The family moved to Duror of Appin from Kinloch Teacuis when his father accepted a position as schoolmaster in Duror school, with a croft at the back of Cuil Bay. For a few years after retiring from teaching, my grandfather was the stationmaster at Keil, on the Ballachulish to Oban railway line. My mother was the only girl in a family of nine and was from Appin. Her father was the local blacksmith "Campbell the Blacksmith" and local farrier. Her mother was a McGillivray from Spean Bridge. Both my parents' pre-war upbringings were crofting-based and hard work. My father had three brothers and two sisters. Alister, Callum and Kirsty all born at Kinloch Teacuis, and Duncan and Flora (Fodie) born at Cuil in Duror after they had moved to the croft at the back of Cuil. My father was the eldest and, as was the custom, shouldered much of the work and responsibility of the croft when his father and mother aged. His father, my grandfather, was an Aberdeen University graduate in modern philosophy. All the children were academically very capable but, as was common at the time, secondary education was a luxury and not everyone was offered a scholarship or a university education when the land needed working.

My mother's brothers were all blacksmiths, having been taught the craft by old man Campbell. He was by all accounts a hard taskmaster. A farrier at Gallipoli with the Argyll Mountain troop, post-WWI he was the North Argyll travelling farrier, often taking the boat from Connel to Glen Etive pier to shoe horses, as well as running the blacksmith's in Appin. He was a good shot, and "Campbell Stew" was a good feed to any visitors who did not mind a bit of poached venison. Sundays would see him take the entire family to church followed by a walk of several miles around North Shian. He would swim, summer or winter, in Loch Creran, and then go into the Creagan Inn for a few drams, leaving the family to walk home. He died of polio, a rather unfitting and unpleasant end for such a robust character, and a reminder, in these Covid times, that mortality from illness pre-vaccination was high. TB in particular took a heavy toll in the Highlands, and sanitoria such as Oban's "Chest Hospital" were still seeing TB patients until the late 1960s.

My father and mother met at a dance in Appin Hall just after WWII. My father had been a prisoner of war and "in the bag" as POWs called it since 1940. Captured at St Valery as part of what felt like the sacrifice of the 51st Highland Division as rear guard and feint, so that Dunkirk could go ahead. This is a forgotten part of the history of the Argylls, Camerons and Norfolk Regiments who made up this division and who were still fighting long after Dunkirk. Many never made it home after capture, being crowded into coal barges sent down canals and rivers, and then a long march into Poland. There, work in salt mines, hard labour and illness, some of which was psychological with men giving up hope and some starvation-related, took its toll. Near the war's end the Wehrmacht tried to move these POWs on what became known as "the long march" escaping the Russians north, where many more perished. When Fiona Campbell met my father, he was about six stone and, like many of his comrades, finding readjusting to normal life difficult. My brother and sisters, like me, witnessed his need to hoard tins of food just in case things ran out. God help you if you dipped into his stash. Both my mother and father were clever and imbued in us a joy of reading and learning. They were, and continue to be, a reminder that as Mark Twain reputedly said, "I didn't get much schooling, so it didn't interfere with my education." Learning, opening your mind and educating yourself does not always need a degree to prove you are clever. I still hold this as truth, as some of the cleverest people I have met were not schooled much, or in some cases labelled "stupid", or what is now known as dyslexic, and had learning needs. They were clever people, but just did not fit into the peg hole of formal education at the time.

My parents were married in Appin Church of Scotland, and Margaret my sister was the first child to come along. Angus (Angie, my brother, also known as "Ben") came along later, both born at Grannie Campbell's in Appin, followed by Kathleen (Kat) born at Glencoe maternity hospital. At the time they lived in "Old Mill" Duror, the end cottage in a group, before turning up to Invernahyle (for a time the Stuart Hotel). These cottages were nicknamed Gomorrah, with the group of two at the top of the hill opposite Duror hall known as Sodom. Who knows why. They had no running water and no electricity, and after a huge flood the family awoke one morning to water lapping at the beds. They applied for a house in a new council house development in Glencoe, in what is now Lorn Drive. Built in 1947, these were Swedish-designed timber houses. My father at that time had several lorries, doing wood haulage from Duror Forest to Kentallen station where it was trained out for use, mainly as pit props in the central belt coal mines. The bigger timber was milled at Duror sawmill, Achindarroch. I came into the world after the move to Glencoe in 1957 and I have not gone that far since. I feel a strong connection with both Duror and Appin, having relatives there to this day, but essentially, I consider myself from Glencoe, even though I popped out into the light in Oban.

My early years at number 15 Lorn Drive, Lower Carnoch, Glencoe, were happy and surrounded by caring neighbours. Macolls and Macfarlanes to one side and Camerons and Mackenzies on the other. These Swedish kit houses were not warm in winter and would creak and move in high winds. Heating was mostly from a range with a built-in oven in the main living room and paraffin heaters. One early recollection is the weekly task of taking a gallon can up the village to "Jock's", the Carmichaels' village shop, and getting the weekly fill of a gallon of paraffin, with any change left over as sweetie money.

As an infant into child I have, as is to be expected, little memory other than what I have been told or gleaned from photographs. As the youngest I came into an already busy family home with the others, so sharing a room with Angie, my brother, was the norm, until he went off to join the

Army. I was pretty sick as a child, getting all the usual rites of passage. Measles, chicken pox and other unnamed viruses. I was extremely ill from measles, and I can remember my parents doing a couple of all-night shifts watching over me as I burned up. As an older child it was whooping cough that was worst, as I ended up with pneumonia and a collapsed lung. I was off school for four months recovering, and I had to have regular visits to the "Chest Hospital" in Oban for X-rays. These visits necessitated a lift to Ballachulish for the 7am early Oban bus, then a taxi up to the old Tuberculosis sanitorium. Naked and cold, ushered into a room with an ancient X-ray machine of wartime vintage, it was a scarring experience, cold, clinical and fear-inducing. Then return by taxi back down to the town, and bus back to Ballachulish with a walk home as my father was at work. I was told that I would not be an active child as I was too weak. The months of antibiotics were almost worse than the illness. My parents were smokers, and I am in no doubt that passive smoking contributed to the illness. It certainly gave me a lifelong and passionate hatred of cigarettes. At a very early age, the weak child remark set me to anger, and I was determined to prove I was anything but. Explains a lot of the drive behind what was to come, perhaps.

School days were at St Mary's Primary School in what is now the church hall next to the Episcopal Church. The school was split into two rooms, the big room for eight- to twelve-year-olds and the wee room for the youngest. When the school moved down to the present building in 1967, somehow the big room/wee room designation stuck. The teachers were memorable and in particular Mrs MacColl, the big room teacher who took no nonsense and drummed the three Rs into us relentlessly. The strap was a last resort but always a present threat if you stepped out of line. School was for rote learning, not fun. In my seven years as a primary school pupil, only once did we get out for something special. This was a sponsored walk to Clachaig to raise money for a trip. Twice, a couple of pupils went on a school cruise on the "Canberra", a school cruise ship, but for most of us pupils from working families, it was not affordable. Occasionally, perhaps every couple of years, we would get a film afternoon when a travelling film man came and we watched something educational, or Pathé News, often something relating to royalty and the fading empire. The teaching did its job, and no one left school unable to read, write and count. An observation looking back to school years was that, apart from the Glencoe Massacre (which was not even given its proper context in Scottish history), very little local or Scottish history was taught.

My sister Margaret, the eldest in the family, was schooled at Duror then Oban High School. I have recollections of going down to the train with my mother at Ballachulish station for her to go to Oban as a weekly boarder and collecting her again on a Friday night. She became a teacher, graduating at Jordanhill, Glasgow. She met my brother-in-law Bernie Walker, who was up staying at what was known as the "Para Hut" (now Bidean Lodge) when he was here on adventurous training with the Army. They married young in Appin Church, then went off to Germany, Hong Kong, Benbecula and Yorkshire. Later she was a senior civil servant in Army budgets. Angie, my brother, joined the Army at only 15 years old as a Junior Leader Royal Corps of Signals and served in many theatres, including tours of Northern Ireland during the worst of the troubles in the 1970s. Kathleen, or Kat as she was known locally, went to St Mary's School Glencoe, as did Angie, then to Kinlochleven and thereafter down to Oban where she trained as a nurse and married, living up at Mossfield for a while before a marriage breakdown and return to Glencoe and back to 15 Lorn Drive with three children. My parents were fortunate to get one of the new builds called "Strathcona Cottages". This allowed my sister to stay at number 15. They qualified because my father was ill with heart disease, having had a heart attack in front of me one night. These houses were built specifically as "Sheltered Housing" or homes for the infirm or sick. Everything on one level, ramp access and emergency cords. It vexes me to see most of them sold off, and some now Airbnbs.

Wanders with a Fishing Rod

In the late 1950s and 1960s, Glencoe was already a busy tourist destination, although nothing like as popular as now. The Glencoe Massacre and the mountains attracted people from all over the world. Crofting was a bigger part of the village life then, and as kids in the summer holidays, helping bring in the hay for a crofter was a way of getting some sweetie money. If you were not an outdoor person, enjoying a bit of fishing or into building gang huts or "bogies" (carts made from pram wheels) or you had no bike, then there was not much in the way of things to do. Television was black and white and mostly an evening entertainment. Village boys and girls were out in all weathers, maybe hanging about at Malloch's shop up next to the village hall, or "Jock's Shop" further down. It was fishing that hooked me. The River Coe at that time was quite a good little river for salmon and sea trout and despite poaching and netting stations, the fish kept on coming, and I was mad keen to catch them. Fishing was rudimentary. None of the arty fly fishing for salmon I do now, just a hook full of worms cast in the right place. I was good at it, very good. I also fly fished, but mainly for brown trout in the local hill lochs such as Loch Ba or up at Bealach near Duror. And I was happy to spend a day out on Rannoch Moor exploring. Often it was only hearing the train on the Bridge of Orchy line that told me that I should walk in the opposite direction to get back to the road for a lift, or the bus that used to run from Tyndrum to Glencoe. We were never short of fish at home, but at times my dad would get frustrated as I would put the big salmon in the bath until I had showed them to friends.

My mother always fretted about me fishing the river when it was in spate (flood) and often came down to make sure I was safe. There were plenty of characters who also fished, and it was fun when the fish were running and folk were catching. Although a small river, one day at the sea pool, 35 salmon and grilse were caught in four hours by various anglers. Another fishing spot was the Glencoe Lochan, which locals knew as "The Lake" and the little ponds below it. Before the road around the Lochan was cleared of rhododendron and the trails were made, this was a wild area largely untouched since Strathcona. Big rainbow, Loch Leven and brown trout were in it. Hard to catch from such a dour, dark, peaty place, but we coaxed them out in the evenings with a worm and float. The boatshed there was the best tryst for a bit of privacy if you had a girlfriend, but it is now sadly gone.

Malloch's shop was run by Charlie and Mary Malloch, and from when I was about eight years old, I would call in and get any fish caught weighed on the counter scales. Malloch's had rows and rows of big old-fashioned sweetie jars behind the serving counter with humbugs, gobstoppers, peanut brittle and other goodies that could be bought by the ounce or pound. A quarter of peanut brittle was my favourite. Also ham and cold meats. Charlie or Mary found it no trouble to stick a sheet of paper on the scales and weigh a big sea trout for me. If catches were good, then a nice plump sea trout was left with them for their teatime (teatime being the Scottish evening meal). Upriver was a favourite fishing spot. I was not in the local angling club at first as I was thought too young to be at the river on my own. My father was an angling club member, although he rarely fished. His membership was eventually transferred to me when I was ten, as long as I had an adult with me, although that seldom happened as I was happier on my own. During summer holidays from school, I would spend dawn till dusk on the river, wandering far, and folk would be sent to look for me if I did not come back for regular meals. The river then, at times, was stuffed with fish and as my tackle was light, it was often broken by large fish. When I say broken, I mean cane and green heart rods I had been given free were snapped into pieces, reel housings ripped off and the line broken. These were big multi sea winter fish which ran early, and they could be well up into double figures in weight.

On one memorable occasion, a very big spring fish led me a merry dance around the tidal pool and decided it was going back down into Loch Leven, stripping 100 yards of line off with me running and wading downriver after it. It passed under the road bridge at Invercoe then turned back upriver but would not move. I spent the next 30 minutes reeling it slowly back up to some trees, finally getting it into my feet at the bank, but with no way of getting it out. So I shouted for help as loud as I could. No one appeared to hear, so I slowly got into the river beside the fish, waist-deep in water, and managed to get it by the tail and hug it and somehow get it out onto the bank, then lift it and run up into Jimmy

Brown the farmer's potato field with it. With great pride and its tail dragging, I walked home with it, enjoying the fame from passing locals and tourists admiring it. I did not realise that the police had been called and folk were searching the river for someone feared drowned as my shouting had been heard. Folk were relieved when word got out it was "just that boy Davy" with a big fish. By my reckoning it was about 18lbs or so, and for an 11-year-old that is a pretty big fish from a spate river. My mother and father worried about me being at the river but just could not stop me as I would sneak out and disappear. I must have worried them sick. This was my Kenn epiphany, similar to that so evocatively written about in Neil Gunn's novel *Highland River*.

Secondary School and Work

On leaving primary school at age 12, we pupils were streamed according to the teacher's opinion of how we would do in secondary school. I was allocated according to that assessment to "G" class, where you had wood and metal work. "C" class was for those more academically gifted. It was, on reflection, nothing more than social engineering, with the children from better-off families going into "C" and working class into "G". The teachers and headmaster were all part of this system. I have few happy memories of Kinlochleven Secondary School. Bullying was rife from both the teachers and out of control older children. Some of the teachers were dysfunctional alcoholics with a penchant for looking up girls' skirts, or mildly psychopathic in their joy at putting fear into children. There were exceptions. The art teacher and English teacher were very kind and invested in their students. The headmaster took a dislike to me from day one until the day I left when only 14 years old, as I could not stand his verbal abuse to me anymore. We were taught about 1066 but nothing of the Union of the Crowns, Jacobites or Red Clydeside. We knew of Cecil Rhodes but not John MacLean, Plato but not Hume. The Battle of the Somme but not of the Braes. Burns was a token subject for limited study every January, although Wordsworth and hosts of golden daffodils were more fitting for our cultural indoctrination. No makars made it into our colonial curriculum.

A bigger impact to my brain at secondary school was getting off the school bus at Corrie Road, Kinlochleven, not realising that below the bus step local kids had created an ice slide, which I went down headfirst and was knocked out. I vaguely recall the pain in my head and the world going dark, then later being sick. After this I remember being shaken by a teacher, having found me asleep with my head on a desk in the class, waking again later in the headmaster's office surrounded by people. A local GP was there and the headmaster. I had a light blue goose down climber's duvet over my back, which I later found out belonged to John Grieve, who was a new and recently qualified teacher in the school. After an hour or so, I was sent to the gym class where I was supposed to be for that period with Mrs Barclay, the gym teacher. I was allowed to sit it out and told I should go home when feeling better. I had a nasty concussion, was sick, nauseous, and I still had to walk to the bus depot 500 metres away. I was the only passenger on the bus. My mother was working, and she found me at home asleep after work that evening. I was sent back to school the following day but could not think or perform anything complex and wanted to sleep all the time. All that got me was a belting for being lazy. As mentioned, I have few fond memories of Kinlochleven Secondary of that time. If there is one blessing, though, it is that many of the kids of my age that I went to secondary school with are still friends and are the saving grace of my two and a bit short years there. That head injury possibly changed my life. Prolonged post-concussion syndrome was not known about at that time, but certainly explains my later difficulties at school and added to an already mounting dislike of the place. I could not think or do anything much and I had dreadful bouts of depression and intrusive suicidal ideation for months after this injury. To be further bullied and treated as stupid was soul destroying. I have a lifelong addiction to learning and personal development and only through the grace of others and their patience did I realise I had some gifts and latent intelligence. That head injury undoubtedly changed my life at a formative period. And yet somehow, just maybe, the later gifts of life came from that nexus. If so, I have to accept these gifts with gratitude.

My parents would have liked me to stay in school, but they could see how unhappy I was. The caveat for me to leave early was to find employment. During weekends and summer holidays, I already had some part-time work. It was kind of a rite of passage for local teen boys and girls to serve petrol at the local Esso garage, which was part of Glencoe Hotel. Owned by the McConacher family, this dilapidated service station was also something of a social hub. There was usually a responsible adult and for each shift a couple of boys out serving at the pumps with the adult taking the cash. My first supervisor was local man called Johnny, known as "The Pilgrim", whom I believe may have been a Rechabite, a temperance movement based on the Old Testament, hence his nickname. He had friends who would sit with him for a blether and to smoke their pipes. I would have to go outside as I hated the fug. Regular baccy puffers would be "Old Rob" and "Old Davie", both full of tales and stories. Old Davie had been about a bit, including working in a chain gang on the Persian Gulf railroad construction. He also worked as a keeper at Mamore Estate and did factory work such as cleaning inside the pipes from the Blackwater Reservoir with a wire brush on a bogie for the British Aluminium company. One memorable story he told was of being caught inside a pipe when the water was put back on, hearing it coming down the pipes and getting out just in time. Another favourite story was the huge snowball that rolled down from Mamore Lodge onto the road with 99 white hares jumping out. To which someone would comment, "Why not just say 100, Davie?" and he would retort that he would not make a liar of himself for one hare. He caught me out one day when discussing salmon. He had been a keen fisherman. He suggested "Jock McBumble" for the reluctant salmon in the pool that season. A bee had to be captured and threaded on a hook and lightly dropped in front of the fish. Thankfully, on capturing a bee in a jar, I never got as far as that cruel manoeuvre, and let it go. Davie and his brother John "Gillenvore" and Jean, their sister, would often be watching me fish from the field above their croft and liked to see what I had caught. Salmon were plentiful and if a fish was caught, a chunk of it would be given to them, and to others in the village.

The service station work was not highly regarded as a full-time occupation, so I was encouraged to move on. Duncan Macdonald had a workshop and joinery business in Glencoe village and my next job was as an apprentice joiner. A few local men were what were called "time served" and good craftsmen. As a new apprentice I was to learn from them. There was nothing formal in this and no studying at college. You just did what you were told and tried to learn. Being a typical hapless immature teenager at barely 15 years old, this was quite a hard world to find my way through. Being a time-served woodworker with an apprentice did not mean being a good and patient teacher, and clouts around the lugs and verbal abuse were very much the order of the day if you made a mistake. Despite that, it had its moments, and I enjoyed working on some of the strange old houses we were sent to, such as on the Island of Lismore. I was sent there once to putty in glass in some new case and sash windows. I was sent across on the Port Appin ferry and picked up by a tractor on the island side. I had to sit in a bucket on the back of the tractor with my big tub of glazing putty and I was taken a long way down the island to do the job. After I had spent all day completing the task, the tractor arrived back to take me to the last ferry to Port Appin. I was back in the bucket at the back of the tractor again. Halfway up the island the bucket was accidentally tipped and I landed on my backside on the road, watching the tractor disappear and with it my chance of getting home that night. Sitting on my sore backside in the winter dusk, I concluded that joinery was not for me.

After two years I left joinery as I had a period of sick absence due to ankle injury sustained running off a mountain. For a short time, I worked at the Shell service station in the village. This was a much more modern service station. I worked a summer there before Tony Cunningham, the local forester for the Forestry Commission, mentioned to my father in the pub that he was looking for some young chaps to start as Forest Craftsmen. The next chapter of my life was also working with wood, but in a way that appealed to me much more. I have great memories from my years with the

Forestry Commission. This was at a time, in the early 1970s, when many of the men who had served their country in WWII were middle-aged and had taken back up the jobs they had left to do their bit. They had war stories to tell, and many were also good naturalists, Gaelic speakers and raconteurs. I spent 14 years with the Forestry Commission. During that time I built fences, planted trees, hauled deer for keepers, tramped the hills of Glenachulish, Duror, Glen Etive and Appin, thinking nothing of going for a hill run around some tops during slack periods. I was mad keen on climbing and running and already in the Mountain Rescue Team that was to form a big part of my life. After five years of general work, I had a Skyline Winch, a felling ticket, and felled and hauled many thousands of tons of timber out of Glen Duror. These were very big trees by Scottish standards and most of the big first and second cuts had to go down to Workington in Cumbria to a sawmill, as nothing in Scotland could mill them. It was also a hazardous job.

One day stacking 3m pulp as a feller (lumberjack) and up to my backside in brash (branches), I was trying to turn a two-ton 4.5m log with a "cant hook", a lever to turn over a log, to get at the underside branches. The lever snapped and I went back downhill, landing on rocks and was knocked out for a few minutes. I woke up with the rain on my face, unable to walk. I crawled to the road where workmates found me. I was heaped in a van and taken home to just above the forest house in Achindarroch, which we rented as part of the job. I tried to walk but ended up crawling down to the house where Fiona found me lying on the floor a few hours later when she came back from teaching skiing. I lay in bed for days and the local GP examined me and thought I had a pelvic fracture. I could not walk without pain for weeks and was on "Fortral" and "Temgesic" (spew in pill form!). Later I was diagnosed with crushed lumbar vertebrae. At this time I was into hard climbing and also serious windsurfing. Within a year my core was strong, but always a simple thing like getting up out of bed too fast and I could be locked up in pain from muscle spasms for days.

On another occasion I took a serious chainsaw cut to my ankle between the Kevlar heel pads of my boots. I also saw a close work colleague getting killed, and in a separate incident a contractor nearby died from a ruptured spleen. It is not just the mountains that are dangerous. Fiona, my wife, was the nearest telephone for any emergencies when we lived at Achindarroch. The fatal accident of a work colleague occurred when we were clear felling as a team in a compartment of mature timber at the top of what was known as "The Cairn Bray" in Duror Forest. Thick tall Sitka timber from a 1919 planting in the two- to three-ton per tree range. The area had hollows and deep dips, and we could not always see each other. The winch was working on an already felled compartment (block of forest) below, with local man Peter Weir on the haul and Neil Black from Appin doing choker (clipping on the logs to haul out). I had gone back to felling and given up the winch, as I had become fed up with the broken ropes from hauling big logs and needed a change.

I could see one of my two closest workmates and I looked over to witness a big tree from a hollow where my other unseen workmate was, buck over, and the tip whip over the man I could see, briefly hiding him under the foliage, then buck back up in the air. My first reaction was he would raise merry hell with whoever felled the tree that covered him and shout blue murder. Sadly, he was down on the ground and not moving, so I ran as best I could through the deep branches. He had been hit on the head and things did not look good. I shouted to Jimmy "the Bush" Cormack, who was doing tally (counting the logs and marking their length and end diameter in a book that gave us an estimated tonnage for daily payment). I got him to jump in the van we had and drive the mile down to our house at Achindarroch and telephone for an ambulance. Fiona was home that day and came back up with him to help me. By that time it was clear it was not a survivable injury, and our close work colleague was dead. The ambulance and police arrived, and he was taken away.

The feller of the tree was in deep shock, especially as it was his closest friend that had been killed. His cut for felling the tree was directional and would have been okay had the tree not come off the stump at the hinge and the wind moved it to the side a fair way off its intended direction of fall. We were too close together though, and with hindsight we had crept well under the two to three tree lengths apart we should have been. These were very big and long trees with four 4.8m logs, a 6.7m smaller diameter log and two 3m pulp wood cuts with a 3m waste top. About 115 feet long. There was something wholesome about a day's hard graft and a pile of timber to show for it. But the physical cost was high. I suppose on the plus side it made me incredibly strong for my size, and I had great endurance. Climbing hard was a great outlet to the grind of hard work too.

Felling was a tough job and very physical. I had no problem being strong for hard climbing as the hard graft from working in the wood kept me lean, strong and fit. But the hard physical work was not good for my temperament. After work on a Friday, a few beers helped. Living up in the woods off the beaten track was a big ask of a young woman recently married, but Fiona was a tough girl and would have made a home and garden in a desert.

Mountaineering Adventures

Childhood, informal education, earning a living, falling in love and getting married young were all interwoven with climbing and mountain rescue.

My early mountain adventures were overshadowed a little by "The Italian Climb", a tragedy on Ben Nevis where four locally based climbers were avalanched. Only one survived. That only survivor, John Grieve, later became Glencoe Mountain Rescue Team leader. His survival was remarkable and needed much fortitude. It is a tale in its own right and the biography of legendary mountaineer Tom Patey by Mike Dixon (Scottish Mountaineering Press) covers the avalanche and rescue in some detail. Events like that loss knock a climbing community backwards, as its heart, the people belonging to the local climbing tribe, are gone. It was in the shadow cast by this tragic event that I somehow got the bug for mountaineering.

The turn of the 1960s into 1970s were overshadowed by that tragic avalanche accident. Then later the death of Tom Patey hit local and Scottish climbers hard. Although he was not a Glencoe local, Patey was a frequent visitor to the area and was often in the village at "Tigh Dearg", Ian and Nikki Clough's house. Or putting out tunes with my uncle, Charlie Campbell, up at the Clachaig Inn. As a boy I saw a slide show on the Old Man of Hoy by Patey in Tigh Dearg. I saw it through a haze of Capstan and Gauloises cigarette smoke and didn't stay long.

Ian Clough sadly lost his life on 30th May 1970 on the British Annapurna expedition led by Sir Chris Bonington, ascending the south face of the mountain. Edinburgh man Dougal Haston and the laconic Don Whillans summited the mountain on 27th May 1970. Bonington later described Ian as "the most unassuming man I ever had the good fortune to climb with".

Ian Clough served in the RAF during his National Service and became part of the RAF Kinloss Mountain Rescue Service. After leaving National Service he ran a small climbing school from Tigh Dearg. One of the best British climbers of his generation, he made many challenging ascents in the Alps. These included the first ascent of the Central Pillar of Frêney on Mont Blanc with Don Whillans, Chris Bonington and Jan Długosz in 1961, and the first British ascent of the north face of the Eiger with Chris Bonington in 1962. He published a guide to Scottish winter climbs in 1969. In 1968, he and Tom Patey became the first to climb Am Buachaille, a sea stack at Sandwood Bay off the coast of Sutherland. Sadly, both Clough and Patey lost their lives in separate climbing accidents within five days of each other. When Clough was killed on Annapurna on 30th May 1970, he would not have known that Patey had met his end while abseiling on 25th May. His wife Nikki Clough climbed the north face of the Matterhorn with Ian and was among the best women mountaineers of her generation. A lovely person who died from cancer at a young age. I was a friend of one of Nikki's nephews, who came up to Glencoe during summer holidays, where we swam in the river most days or fished. Little did I know I was rubbing shoulders with mountaineering legends when in Tigh Dearg. They certainly inspired me and got me hooked on climbing. Patey's death through lack of attention to safety on the "Maiden" sea stack in northwest Scotland took away a climbing legend and character. Although a great mountaineer, he could be reckless, and a bit cavalier. The mountains do not forgive complacency, especially in the form of an old carabiner used to hold your trousers up. He used no safety backup system such as is taught nowadays for abseiling. The old plain carabiner without a locking gate twisted itself off the abseil device when he leaned back. Hamish MacInnes, who gave him the carabiner, warned him it was unsafe and not to be used when climbing.

Tigh Dearg, the climbers' house, was 150 metres up the road from my family's house at 15 Lorn Drive, Glencoe. Before getting married, Fiona and I made an offer to buy Tigh Dearg from Nikki, but at £11,500 it was too much on our meagre wages at the time. The Bathgate family, Andrew, Dave and Doug, bought the cottage, and it remained very much a mountaineers' house for a long time after.

By the mid-1970s I was tentatively finding my way into harder climbing. I often struggled with the reputation of some of the Glencoe climbs, many of which were the classic test pieces of their day. Dave Knowles, a local climber who was living in a flat at Invercoe House, gave me some advice one day when I was in the Clachaig having a beer. He told me to go climbing in England for a long spell and then come back to Glencoe. This would give me an opportunity to climb on many different types of rock and get me away from the spell cast by the harder Glencoe routes. It was very good advice. Dave was sadly killed by a falling rock during the making of the film *The Eiger Sanction* starring Clint Eastwood. Another tragic loss to the local climbing community and more dark clouds, with questions of why we love the mountains and climbing. Mistakes and errors of judgement are dealt with harshly by gravity and geography in the mountains.

In these early years I had some adventures. One particular youthful folly was a bit embarrassing when I was rescued along with three others by the Glencoe rescue team.

Euan Grant, a friend, had called in to say we were going up the hill with a couple of his brother's friends. Typical teenager, still in bed at 9.30am, I was far from ready. They collected me at about 10am and said it was just to be a quick trip up into Ossian's Cave. Ossian's Cave is a place of some local history and folklore. Nicol Marquis, a local shepherd, climbed into it in 1868. This was verified by some Scottish Mountaineering Club members years later. They found a rag he had tied to a tree up at the cave. Ossian was, as legend has it, a warrior-poet born in the cave.

The legend of Ossian and these bardic tales also say that earlier in history a girl, Sadbh, was turned into a deer by the druid Fer Doirich, and then hunted by the warrior Fionn (Finn McCool of Irish legend). Fionn caught the deer but did not slay her, and Sadbh was transformed back into her natural form. From this encounter she became pregnant with Ossian, who was born in the cave. It is a nice mythical story, but I am pretty sure Nicol Marquis was first into the cave. I say cave, but it is really just a sloping ramp of moss, sedum and rock.

On our adventure we had wet feet from crossing the river, and then we had a long slog up the steep scrambly path to the ramp at the foot of the cave. We arrived around 12.30pm. The weather was very cold, frosty and dry, although the forecast was for some wintry weather coming in later. After much faffing around, one of the party made his way up to the cave which, as mentioned, is not really a cave but more a steep grassy festival of mountain vegetation and rowan trees with some rock thrown in, making it appear like a rock climb. Not a place to fall off, but not technical if you don't mind pulling up on rock and mixed vegetation.

We all climbed to the cave in turn. This took a while and at about 3.30pm it was dusk and getting dark. Everything around us was freezing water ice, but no snow. In the poor light we missed the exit ramp off below the cave and ended up going further north. Our lights were very poor by modern comparison. A single ordinary torch bulb, no halogen bulbs or LED lights back then. The head torches we carried were wired to a small square blue "Ever Ready" cardboard-encased battery, with two terminals. It lit up your feet but had no beam to throw out in front to see for any distance, or down into big drops. We ended up in a steep ice-filled gully. I was lowered to the end of the rope, which had run out, and with a huge black drop below me, the game was up. I was very cold. Luckily for me my father had just been paid £800 redundancy money from the Forestry Commission engineering department. He gave each of us kids some money to buy something. My choice was a goose down "Annapurna" duvet jacket. I knew the price of the duvet from seeing it on an earlier visit to Nevis Sport in Fort William. I went to the post office for postal orders to the value and sent off a letter ordering my duvet jacket. That was on a Monday. We needed rescuing the following Sunday. On the Friday before our misadventure, the duvet was delivered by hand, I think by one of the Knowles brothers who had gone across the Ballachulish Ferry and into Fort William for something at Nevisport. Nevisport at that time was at the west end of Fort William in an old dairy building, often with a big husky peering at you from the flat roof above the entrance door. Many local climbers and mountain rescuers worked there over the years. Willie Stitt from Killin worked there around the time I bought the duvet, and the shop owners were Ian Sykes and Ian Sutherland, who had returned from working on the British Antarctic Survey. Later, local man Alec Gillespie managed the shop for them. It was fortuitous that my new duvet arrived quickly as it probably saved my life, or at least held off more serious hypothermia.

On the night in question, I climbed back up the rope and then we talked out a plan. We thought that we could sit out the night, which is very long and dark in the mid-November Highlands. After a few uncomfortable hours, it started to lightly snow and became very cold. We had on our lights. A couple of cars came into Achtriochtan farm below, one of which flashed its lights up at us. I was pretty sure my father (and as it turned out, my mother) would be up for a look and very worried. After discussion we decided not to flash back and stay put. After another long period we were getting very cold. Another car pulled in and flashed. We flashed back six flashes with the one torch left working. We also decided to move back up to a bigger ledge, although we could not see the farm from it. After a while, a vehicle could be seen coming up the A82 but could not be seen going further up the Glen, so we assumed it could be the rescue team. After what seemed like hours, the remaining torch which Euan had was dim and we were worried about not being seen. It was then that Euan said he had a flare in his rucksack which he had taken from his brother John's boat. John did not know he had taken it. Euan was understandably reluctant to use it.

Unbeknown to us, it was a parachute flare. Euan took it out, pulled the striker and mistakenly had it pointing downhill as he had the striker end up near his head torch to see the firing instructions. When it went off a big red streak was followed by a bang and a red flash exploded below, and we could see figures diving for cover. Then it was pitch black again. Sometime later Wull Thomson arrived with a search light. It was a car battery on a pack frame on his back wired up to a car headlight. Walter Elliot arrived, chirpily saying, "Hi, Davy, how's it going?" in his wry way, and so did Hamish. After some discussion, finding a good way down was delegated to Walter, who gathered sheep from around Ossian's Cave in places mountaineers would fear to tread. He led us up onto a ledge and back onto the ramp. We then followed him down the animal track that cuts below "Findlay's Rise", a winter ice climb, and down to the Coire nan Lochan footbridge. I have used this route since, and it's an exciting but easy adventure on a good narrow path among steep terrain. If you can find it. Which is not easy from above, as the entrance looks very difficult and intimidating. All it requires is a bum slide around a steep bit then you are on a descending ramp. Intimate knowledge such as Walter's is crucial to mountain rescue. Shepherds and stalkers have always played a big part in rescue from the Scottish mountains.

We went down to the river, and then toiled back up the interminable slope, what locals called the "Pipers" car park, on the A82. Everyone waiting was just glad we were okay and there was no slagging off. Lifts were offered, thanks proffered, and I was whisked home by Sandy Whellans, the local police sergeant. I was extremely cold. I went into my parents' house to find neighbours in to visit and offer support. Gaiters and boots were removed along with wet clothes, and down to my undies, I got ushered off to a hot bath and then to bed. I awoke in the morning to a foot of fresh snow and a strong wind outside my bedroom window. I was very glad not to be still up at the cave. It took a few days to get an underlying coldness to pass, a feeling of literally being cold to my core, with bouts of shivering and extreme tiredness. Villagers were not critical of us, just glad we were okay. My parents later revealed the helplessness and fear they felt seeing our lights up on that dark north face. I have had a few adventures over the years and met some very interesting people. Experience is nothing more than a sum of all the mistakes you make. What follows in this book is a bit of insight into life in a mountain community, some of the people and adventures. Also herein a few tales of mountain rescue, and of course a bit more on Hamish, who was such a colourful character to be around.

A Guide's Tale

My early climbing was full of anxiety and fear. I loved it and was scared stiff in equal measure. Such were the local legends of the sport and their tales that I felt like an imposter into such a world. I was full of self-doubt and feelings of inadequacy, and put-downs by the legends were not in short supply. I quickly realised that I had to shut up and apply the adage "train hard – fight easy". I would boulder in boots, secretly go running and cycling, and do weights. Harder climbs felt easier if you had scared yourself shitless on some esoteric choss heap where no one else would dare go. Eventually some confidence came. Enough to think I might one day become a mountain guide like my heroes Lionel Terray or Giusto Gervasutti. My early guiding attempts soon disabused me of that. I will admit that I probably felt an imposter for most of my 53 years climbing, rescuing and mountaineering, but I learned to mask it. Sometimes overcompensating by appearing bolder than I really am on long, scary runouts or difficult conditions. The internal battle was often greater than the physical difficulty.

By the time I was nearly 18, I had climbed quite a lot, I had been rescued, and I had helped on many rescues. I was gaining experience. Perhaps much of that was bad experience. Mountain guiding was still mainly confined to a few climbers within the Glen, with these few mostly in the employ of the old fox Hamish, or others from Hamish's "Glencoe School of Winter Mountaineering". Many were employed on an ad hoc basis, recruited when mountain instruction was in demand. Notables were the likes of Alan Fyffe and Kenny Spence.

As I was walking down the village one Saturday, a passing car stopped. The driver wound down his window and asked if I knew of a local guide for hire. A couple of names were passed to him, and the chosen route asked. When the reply came that it was none other than "The Gully" (Clachaig Gully, a classic climb), I felt compelled to offer my services – for a reasonable fee of course. I was a mere youth, not yet tempered by trying real hard men's climbs like Shibboleth. One climb above all was revered by us fresh-faced youths, both from behind and in front of the public bar at Clachaig. This was partly out of convenience. Like the hindquarters of an elephant, as eloquently described by Bill Murray, it started only ten minutes from the bar door. "The Gully" could be done either solo before 12.30 Sunday opening or roped between 2.30 and 6.30pm, usually by a mixed company of barman/maid and customer. It is fair to say "The Gully" was well known to us.

I was hired, but not before my clients revealed that they were a professional couple, betrothed, and in addition they belonged to a "socialist mountaineering club" (The Red Rope Walking and Climbing Club) and as such were happy to support the local proletariat although not at excessive cost. We settled on a less than princely sum, perhaps due to my obvious youth and assumed lack of experience. I went home to collect my climbing gear.

My kit at that time was by modern standards very meagre. Turning 17 years old in May, it was only three months since my birthday. Dances, ceilidhs and girls took priority for my spending. So it was that I, as a junior Bergführer, assembled my meagre rack of gear at the foot of the gully. A 200ft No 2 Viking nylon donated by Robin Turner, a local climber, after an abseil lesson from him off his cottage roof. I had a pair of Lionel Terray leather mountain boots, and I had the most modern harness of its time, the ubiquitous "Whillans Harness". These and a set of nuts made by clog attached to wire hawser, a selection of pitons and several slings in bright pink tape concluded the ironmongery for the ascent. It had not rained for a month, but nevertheless it would not have occurred to me to wear rock boots, even though I had a pair of EBs donated to me by Sandy Whellans, the local policeman. The Gully is a boot climb. That's how W.H. Murray did it on its first, and how it was done on subsequent ascents by early pioneers, and you always follow in the footsteps of the masters, don't you?

We started the Gully at its lowest point via a pitch shown to me only the Sunday before by one of the barmen. This pitch is walked past by most climbers, but I thought that as I was getting paid for the job in hand, then a refund might be requested should all available rock not be included in the ascent. It went well, with the pair climbing very fast and very competently in parallel on twin No 2 weight Viking nylon ropes. During conversation it became clear that proper guides were hired on a regular basis by the couple. Indeed the previous weekend a "proper" guide had been secured in the Llanberis Pass for the same rate as I, and three of the classics of the pass, including the renowned "Wrinkle", had been successfully ascended.

The haze of morning had become a menacing black shroud of afternoon cloud, and soon the occasional very large plop of rain fell. By this time we had passed the lower greenery and were in the more austere surroundings of the crux slab above the "Great Cave". The atmosphere was oppressive and clearly it was going to become very wet. We passed a road sign saying "ice" complete with metal post, put there the previous year by some pranksters on a university freshers' weekend. The slab was climbed and soon we were at the redoubtable "Jericho Wall", which at that time was pitch eight of the roped pitches if you include the lowest pitch. I regaled them with stories of derring-do, and an account of the early history of the Gully, plus, of course, a few rescue stories to enhance the atmosphere. It clearly had the desired effect, as they were keen to push on and seemed apprehensive to say the least. This was further heightened when the rain started, and we realised we were in for a deluge.

The pressure was on, but could the aspirant Bergführer pull it out the bag without needing the services of the rescue team? Absolutely. Afterburners on, it was all go with each subsequent pitch dispatched at full speed and a full-blown thunderstorm breaking around us. With the prospects of drowning and falling as a combined incentive, the pair climbed well, despite being visibly terrified, so all credit to them as I was feeling a burden of responsibility well beyond my young years. We topped out after a five-hour ascent, 30-odd pitches, over 1,700 feet of climbing and in a reasonable time for a roped party of three. Some parties have taken upwards of 14 hours and, in one case, two full days. For us, all that remained was the knee-wrecker down to the pub and a beer by the fire. That path down is steep and tortuous and requires a bit of care. A bedraggled crew, we arrived at the pub safely two hours later. They reluctantly bought me a beer as I was underage but complimented me on a fine though short day. As the day was shorter than their climbing in the famous Llanberis Pass, and the Gully deemed inferior, and having discussed the fee, they felt that it should be halved. So it was barely enough cash for an evening "session" that was handed over to the naive Bergführer, who there and then decided that the people's flag was not as red as thought. Guiding might not be for him after all.

Fiona

I first saw Fiona on an Icelandic pony, Venga, riding bareback through Glencoe village with her sister Pandy on her horse, Meshoni (christened Angela, but the nickname Pandy stuck). I was struck by this attractive blonde girl who looked wild and interesting. On meeting her at the tidal pool one day, I did not hesitate to ask her on a date. The date consisted of a walk to Clachaig and a pint of cider for her and beer for me. I had, it seemed, met a girl/woman who did not want to be tamed but was up for anything adventurous and always had a huge laugh and big smile, even when halfway up Clachaig gully in a deluge.

She was just 17 when we met. Six months later we were engaged, then in November 1978 we married in St Mary's Church, Glencoe, then moved into a Forestry house at Achindarroch, Duror. During our courtship and after, I was very involved with the Mountain Rescue Team. Fiona also came and helped on many rescues, although sometimes she was not made very welcome by some of the older members, one of whom told her he came on rescues to get away from his wife, and it was no place for a woman! As she had climbed some of Glencoe's hardest climbs and the complainant was no climbing star, it seemed particularly ironic, but although it hurt for a bit, it didn't bother her for long. She became a highly competent mountaineer, summer and winter, sharing a rope most often with me. She also climbed with many friends who went on to be IFMGA guides, or already had the guide carnet. A reliable belayer and competent mountaineer, she was a good companion on a rope.

The norm after marriage back then was "leave and cleave". You were expected to make your bed and lay on it come what may. After a very brief honeymoon, as we had little money, we moved into the house at Achindarroch. I was working in the wood, she was making prawn creels for local fisherman Bob Hamilton and Jan, his partner, or serving tables at Ardsheal House or Duror Inn of an evening. With no car at first, we either walked to Agnes and Innes Macoll's shop two miles away or, once a week, the travelling grocer Bill McCubbin called up and we resupplied. We had some tough winters during these first years, often getting snowed in. We eventually bought a car and although we only had provisional licences, we drove everywhere until Fiona passed her test. She taxied me to the pub, to rescues, and was more patient and accommodating than I should ever have asked. An absolute star. We had married young and had a lot of fun in our twenties. Good friends as well as a married couple. After 12 years together, we decided to start a family. She blossomed from the vivacious, attractive, untameable public school girl into a strong, confident and strikingly beautiful woman, both in spirit and outward looks. Looks she most often shunned in preference to old clothes and having her hands in the soil, gardening.

I count myself lucky to have married her, as she kicked me up the backside and helped make me whatever it is I became and which you may read about from here on. Never ceasing to encourage and cajole, she supported me in mountain rescue, climbing and all aspects of my life. It was she who recognised I had a good brain and should go into adult education. I ended up with bits of paper proving to myself I wasn't stupid, having passed exams, and I even became a member of the Royal College of Surgeons as a founder of the faculty of prehospital care. When I received my MBE for services to Mountain Rescue, I always thought it was Fiona and the three children's award much more than mine. I have a dislike of titles but accepted the honour for my family's sacrifice, and it is my acknowledgement to them for their support of me.

Glencoe Classic Climbs

Thinking about rock climbing routes that inspired me, or made an impact on my climbing, be it good or bad, many were in Glencoe. Although I climbed extensively elsewhere in the UK, the Glencoe routes were formative for me as a young man, as they often represented a psychological barrier, as well as being physically demanding. There are quite a lot of routes to sift through and many of the most enjoyable routes have been notable not by epic days or hard grades, but by the people I have shared them with. I have always loved climbing in the Lake District and the Peak District as well. I have done a lot of climbing in North Wales too, although as someone from a Gaelic culture, I always struggled a bit with the attitude of some of the locals in North Wales, as it was so out of keeping with what I was used to. One example being people speaking in Welsh to us when they knew we could not understand. I had not come across that here in the Gaelic-speaking Highlands, where hospitality and courtesy were part of the culture. I liked Clogwyn Du'r Arddu on Yr Wyddfa, but always felt intimidated on the sea cliffs of Gogarth, climbing above the sea!

There just isn't space to cover all the Glencoe routes that made an impression or were just good fun regardless of grade. I will only mention some of the Glencoe classics at the top of the Very Severe graded list from yesteryear. The ones I literally grew up on after climbing the easier classics like Clachaig Gully, Agags Groove, Archer Ridge and many others. Some routes, especially when I was a young man, were surrounded by myth and an aura of impregnability, or in one case the psychological barrier was that I had been on two fatal rescues on the route where leaders had fallen and been killed. It took me some time to have the courage to climb "Big Top" on E Buttress Aonach Dubh. It is an absolutely stunning big mountain rock climb with outstanding situations, and technically not too hard at all, just very exposed. I even managed the pitch that had claimed leaders' lives in a heavy drizzle. The sense of elation at finally laying that itch to rest was pretty heady. Climbing Trapeze, Big Top and Hee Haw in succession late on a sunny evening while the sun dipped into the northwest in a mid-June heatwave gave the very best of Glencoe rock one evening a few years later.

Much of our early climbing in Glencoe relied on the Scottish Mountaineering Club (SMC) guidebooks and their graded lists. Volume 1 Buachaille Etive Mòr and Glen Etive, and Volume 2 Glencoe and Ardgour.

The early Glencoe climbs were graded from Moderate to Severe, then later Very Severe was added. Very Severe remained the hardest technical grade in Scottish guidebooks for nearly 80 years. As climbs received ascents, word of mouth would spread information as to a climb's falling-off potential, and the likely result of injury or death. The grade reflected how technically hard a crux, the hardest climbing move and often the point of no return on a climb, was. To indicate the very hardest of each grade of route, a graded list was compiled at the back of a guidebook, with the hardest and most serious routes at the top and the easier routes at the bottom. The list was supposedly based on consensus. But being subjective and at the whim of egos, this could result in anomalies. No climber liked to admit a route was desperately hard for them, and so some climbs were placed much further down the graded list than they should have been. Climbers had a term for routes that were harder than the grade, calling them "sandbags". The unwary leader could find themselves shaking from fear with legs vibrating (known as the sowing machine leg) and have to dig deep. Until 1980 even the most extreme mountain routes in Glencoe were still only graded at Very Severe.

I worked my way up through the graded lists with various partners, and as the climbing season went on, I became fitter, better technically and stronger mentally. This made me more confident. The other guidebooks of the time were Hamish MacInnes's guides with his own unique and slightly dubious grading system. We often chose Hamish's book for a picture and the SMC guides for the route description. Ken Crocket's guidebook to Glencoe, published in 1980, had much improved route descriptions and topographic picture guides to the climbing routes. The new guide included a modern revised grading system, including extremely severe for seriousness and a numerical technical scale representing technical difficulty.

You can tell which routes were important to me in my old guidebooks, as a page was torn out and then taped back in for hard climbs like Shibboleth. I first became aware of this shortcut to carrying a guidebook while doing Jaywalk on the Etive Slabs with friend George Reid when he took a guidebook page out of his pocket. Often we would just write out the route description, but when it was a big scary route, the page came out of the book.

The hard rock routes of Glencoe all had an aura about them from the legends who did the first ascents and were shrouded in mystery. The names Smith, Marshall, Cunningham and Whillans were legends, as were Dougal Haston and Dave Bathgate. Also, home-grown climbing heroes such as Wull Thomson and John Hardy with their route, Kingpin. Ian Nicholson was a legend, with fast winter solo ascents of Point Five Gully and Zero Gully, before a few lunchtime beers in the Jacobite bar, Fort William. His soloing of rock routes, including jumping over a falling leader's ropes while soloing on the Etive Slabs were legendary.

There are also climbing routes that are memorable because they have stood the test of time for sheer bloody awkwardness, and the stamina needed despite their short length. Bloody Crack, or Raven's Gully in summer. Marshall's Wall on Gearr Aonach for boldness, or Valkyrie and Tous les Deux on the Etive Slabs for route finding and scary long leads up blank slabs. Lechers/Superstition or Bludgers/Revelation on the Buachaille's slime wall stand out as fantastic route combinations in outstanding situations. Or the underrated Marshall route "Apparition" on slime wall, which is the equal of Shibboleth in quality, if a little easier.

Trapeze. Fiona and I awoke at Achindarroch Duror one sunny Saturday morning in June 1984 wondering what we should do with our day. From somewhere the notion to go up onto Aonach Dubh and E Buttress and to climb Trapeze E1 5b 500ft was decided on. First climbed by Jimmy Marshall and Derek Leaver in 1958, it is a classic three-star Glencoe climb, with the further excellent routes of Big Top to its left and Hee Haw over to the right. We sorted out gear for the climb and loaded up our Vauxhall Chevette. A couple of weeks before, between the two of us, we had taken out the engine of this car with a Tirfor winch and pulleys up between two trees. We had the engine rebored and having taken it apart, we also put it back together again. Fiona was a dab hand at setting points and timing with her own strobe. She also rebuilt the carburettor. Her mechanical nous came from her dad, who loved car tinkering as a classic car enthusiast.

We went up to Glencoe, parking at Elliot's bridge, Achnambeithach. Then came the long toil up the lower approach to the middle ledge of Aonach Dubh's west face, followed by an airy traverse to below E Buttress. Two pairs of climbers were already on the climb Big Top when we arrived at the foot of the buttress. Gearing up and climbing fairly quickly, I went up the well-protected corner of Trapeze and brought up Fiona, who had taken her Olympus OM-1 camera, carried on a sling over her shoulder. The OM-1 was a metal body SLR and famed for its robust build and excellent lens. Sadly, it took a bump, and the lens wouldn't focus, so we had no pictures that day. I then climbed the next pitch, which was a bit more broken, arriving in a mossy corner that was airy and full of atmosphere. The next pitch was up the side of the slab where we in the rescue team had recovered the body of a young lad. This was only three years earlier and still fresh in my mind. The lad killed was on Big Top, climbing on twin 9mm ropes. He went off route on the final pitch of Big Top and fell 100 feet onto the Trapeze slab when one of his two ropes had parted. It was possibly acid from the exposed battery in the back of a minivan. The old minivans had the battery behind the seat and if not covered over by its lid, it was a hazard. That memory didn't detract from our day as we were having fun, and you learn to firewall such memories. Next came my favourite pitch, up well-protected cracks to the buttress's highest point. Laced with good protection, it's a sensational pitch and overhangs slightly at the top. I had tugged in a wire nut just below the top of the pitch, where it slightly overhangs. Fiona couldn't get it out despite many tries and using a nut key to jab it. A lot of cursing and colourful language echoed around the crag while she tried. Fortunately, in the end she was successful. And knackered with pumped-out forearms.

We went up to the buttress top, coiled the ropes alpine-style over our backs, and then descended down the ramp at the side of the buttress. The descent is a down climb with a tricky rock step where if you fell off, you would be a goner. We were not roped at this point but maybe should have been. I always felt protective towards Fiona in situations like that, but she was very competent and would have asked for a rope if she needed it. She wasn't one for caring about losing face and climbed for fun, not ego. If she wanted a rope, she would definitely ask. Gear was packed away then we went back along the middle ledge. We hadn't gone far along the ledge when we heard the sound of a motor bike screaming down the A82. We looked for the rider on the road and saw the rider come off, followed in seconds by the sound of a big bang. Later a police car arrived, but no ambulance, so we took it the rider wasn't injured. Quite a sight from high on a cliff.

We arrived down at the car and went to Clachaig for a beer. At the bar were climbers telling the barman about this woman cursing on Trapeze. We admitted it was us, and we had a good laugh with them about the colourful language. They were miners out on strike from a colliery in Yorkshire, at the time of Thatcher's breaking of the miners' unions. After a cold beer it was then off back home to get the chainsaw sharpened and clothing ready for next day in the wood, cutting trees. A fairly typical Sunday for us in the 1980s when every Saturday and Sunday were climbing days if it was dry weather somewhere in Scotland. I went back to E Buttress many times in the years that followed. Hee Haw is relatively easy, but what makes it good as a climb are the giant blocks and overhanging nature of the route, which is slightly outrageous.

Hamish MacInnes, in conversation, recalled filming Hee Haw's second ascent with Robin Smith and another unnamed climber. They were short of a second climber for the film. Robin noticed a young lad camped at Clachaig had a rope beside his tent. Robin asked him if he'd like to go on a climb. The boy was keen, but he only had plimsoles for his feet.

The night before, Robin had slept on Hamish's floor at Allt na Ruigh, his old home. During the night Robin's sleeping bag burst and feathers got out. Robin and the house were covered in down. The trio made it up to the bottom of Hee

Haw, Robin leading. Then, when safe, they belayed up the plimsole man, who became stuck at the crux of the climb on the first pitch, which is quite low down. Hamish had to go help him, leaving his camera gear below the climb. He later found a good position to film the climb and mentioned he still had the film somewhere. Hamish took a frame from the film to use on an obituary of Robin, who was killed in the Pamirs. Hamish described it as a wonderful picture showing Robin with some goose down clinging to his grandmother's cardigan, which he was wearing on the day.

Hee Haw is fun, but the best route on this buttress, in my opinion, is Big Top, which wends and weaves its way up the buttress and has truly outstanding views and climbing. Maybe one of the best E1 mountain climbs in the UK. Doing all three routes in a day, finishing at sunset, a quick swim in the River Coe, then a cold beer at Clachaig all add to a memorable day.

Unicorn. In the summer of 1982, Bernard Newman, editor of *Climbing*, one of the UK's most popular climbing magazines, was working on a book for the series started by Ken Wilson. The classic coffee table book *Hard Rock* had been out for a while and introduced many to the delights of the best harder climbs in Scotland, England and Wales. *Hard Rock* was then followed by *Classic Rock*. Now there was to be a book called *Extreme Rock*. Bernard and Janine, his wife, were good friends of Ed and Cynthia Grindley, a climbing couple who were living in Glencoe village, where at that time Cynthia was the district nurse.

I had first met Ed Grindley in 1975 when he was working for Glencoe School of Winter Mountaineering, staying at Tigh Dearg, the climbers' house on the village street. We had a few adventures climbing and on winter rescues, and he liked to party. As a Lakeland climber of some note, Ed was established as one of the best rock climbers of the time. His organised approach to climbing gear preparation and training had quite a significant impact on me. Pre-Friends, the camming devices from Wild Country, nuts were the only thing for protection. Banging in pitons or pegs, as we called them, had become unnecessary. It was a blessing not having a hammer and jangly, heavy bits of steel banging about on a harness or bandolier. Ed often carried two full sets. Chouinard Stoppers 1–10 in full sizes on one side of a harness, and 1–10 in half sizes on the other. He also epoxied the wires into the end of the nut so they could be fangled in and out without the wire pushing through. These and sets of hexes for camming into cracks. I can remember him gluing thicker pieces of canvas to the heels of his EBs (these were a type of rock climbing shoe) to give more edge support and carefully cleaning his rock boot soles for maximum grip. I was impressed by his pre-climbing preparation and he introduced me to training for climbing in a more serious and planned way.

One of my earliest climbing trips with Ed was in 1976 and involved going to Wales. We went via Aviemore and the Cairngorms as we wanted to do the classic climb, "The Needle", on the Shelter Stone before going south. This trip included Ronnie Rodger, another local-born lad who is a bit older than me. Ronnie also got the climbing bug at a very young age and was in the rescue team.

When we arrived at the Cairngorm chairlift, it was hellish windy. Ronnie and I set off up the chairlift with the ropes while Ed faffed about at his van. We got to the top to be told the chair was closing due to the wind. Having no idea if Ed was on the chairlift and with no sight of anyone else looking back down the line, we pleaded to get back to the bottom. Halfway down we met Ed on the way up, having pleaded his case to get on to join us. Thankfully, he was allowed to come back down again by the lifty, who took pity on him at the top. The lifty happened to be John MacLean, one of the best climbers of an earlier generation. It was an inauspicious start to a day's climbing. We decided to go into Newtonmore for a few pints. We then drove down to Dunkeld and soloed some routes such as Ivy Crack, Poison Ivy and some others. I still had on my big Fitzroy leather boots.

We stayed the night at Ed's in Bannockburn where he and Cynthia lived before getting married and moving to Glencoe. The next day we travelled down to Llanberis in Ed's van and stayed at the Fell and Rock Club's climbing hut at Ynys Ettws in Llanberis Pass. What followed was a week of baking hot sunshine, drought and pubs with no beer. I played darts with legends Joe Brown and Don Whillans and met many of the best climbers and legends of the day on that trip.

It was with Ed that this next climbing adventure took place. Stob Coire nan Lochan in Glencoe has some quite good routes among its teetering blocks and well-known classic winter routes. Two of these routes were to feature in *Extreme Rock*. Scansor, a Tut Braithwaite route, was to be in the book. It had received a second ascent by Paul Nunn and Ian Nicholson (I think). Unicorn was the other route. First climbed in 1967 by Jimmy Marshall and Robin Campbell. Jimmy was a legend of Scottish mountaineering in both summer and winter, making at least 100 first ascents. He had a very good eye for climbing lines, and the majority of the routes he recorded (who knows how many he deemed unworthy) were to become classic climbs. His Glencoe legacy on Buachaille Etive Mòr includes Crest Route – Left Edge in 1956, graded Severe, and which will scare the pants out of the average Severe leader although an excellent climb on perfect rock. Finding Bludgers route link into Revelation in 1957, Lechers Superstition in 1959 and the excellent and little known Apparition in 1959 as well as Trapeze on Aonach Dubh in 1958, and on the Etive Slabs, the classic route Pause in 1960. And later this route Unicorn, climbed in 1967. He was also a legendary winter mountaineer and an incredibly good writer. His Scottish Mountaineering Club Journal writings "Garde De Glace" and "The Orion Face" should be read by any aspiring winter climber.

Unicorn had perhaps about half a dozen ascents before we climbed it for the book. At least that I knew of. Both of these routes, due to lack of climbing traffic, had some very loose rock, especially at the top of Unicorn. On the day of the climb, we arrived at the Pipers layby, the upper car park for Stob Coire nan Lochan. It was so called as back then a certain Mr MacPhee in full Highland regalia, including bearskin hat, would ply his trade playing his bagpipes there. Play might be too kind a word for what came out the pipes, but he plied his skirl to advantageous effect. He had a wee table set out with a bowl for donations, and another with some lucky white heather. His wife or daughter would be nearby in an old van.

Ed and I travelled up together ahead of the others. At that time Ed had a bright orange RS Cosworth Ford Escort. He thought it might be a laugh to go a bit fast and handbrake stop just before the piper. Although he stopped in time, the piper MacPhee, on diving for cover, went over the bank. We went to help him back up and apologise and were on the receiving end of much cursing and swearing. He appeared unharmed apart from his attire being all over the place. We grabbed our kit to get away and MacPhee hurled a "Buidseachd" or curse at us in Gaelic, shouting "One of you will not come back here today."

Not the best start to a day's climbing. Ed, Cynthia, Bernard, Janine and I slogged up the grinding path to the corrie, which back then hadn't been made into the climber's superhighway of stepped path it is now. It has always been a grind up that path with ropes and a heavy rucksack, and the new steps don't lessen that.

Scansor was the first route we did with Ed leading the crux and Cynthia and I following. Ed was taking some pictures with a compact camera, and Bernard had an SLR on a tripod in the corrie. Scansor was a bit mossy and the technical crux overlooking SC gully was airy but okay. The rest of the route was a bit broken and loose. Not a great route in my opinion, but okay if you're up there anyway. We went along the top of the cliffs and then came back down forked gully, looking for climbing gear dropped into the snow and lost by the many dozens of climbers going that way in winter. We found some swag, mostly pitons, and a single glove. Next was an ascent of Unicorn by Ed and me. I led up and belayed in the corner, avoiding the normal belay. We wanted to try and climb the route in three pitches. Ed led through on our twin 150ft ropes. He was high in the corner near the end when I heard him shout and looked up to see three big slabs of rock heading down the corner towards me. I had no helmet on, and nowhere to go. One missed my head and glanced off my shoulder, chopping a belay sling. One missed me, but the other passed down my chest, hitting my ankle, and then off down to the corrie. The sulphurous smell from rockfall hung about a bit. My shoulder was badly bruised and cut but not, it seemed, broken. The same shoulder had been hurt in the past from crashing a motor bike. My ankle was really sore and already swelling. Ed went into self-rescue mode, but I thought I was okay, and it would be much easier to finish the route if I could. With the adrenaline hit I was able to climb up to the top, then hobble down forked gully again. Bernard had one hellish fright watching this unfold through his camera lens and was a bit shaken up. Given the size of the rocks, he thought I had no chance. It was just sheer luck I didn't get one square on the head. I doubt a helmet would have helped, but that's no excuse. I made my way slowly down to the car. The piper was gone by the time we had made it back to the road. He might well have smiled had he seen me hobbling and a bit bloody.

We went back to Ed's house in the village as I had arranged for Fiona to meet us there and take me back home to Duror where we lived. She was already in Ed and Cynthia's house waiting. Ed went in ahead of me and said to her "I nearly killed your husband today." Bernard got his pictures and story, and the book *Extreme Rock* was a considerable success, including our climbs in it. While Unicorn is undoubtedly a great route and Scansor okay, they were curious choices for the book, in my opinion. I understood that some of the classics like Shibboleth had been covered in *Hard Rock*, but I think Ed's own route, the Clearances, or Pete Whillance's the Risk Business would have been better choices to represent the grade jump of the early 1980s.

This was also a time when Dave "Cubby" Cuthbertson and Murray Hamilton, along with other climbers, made a quantum leap in climbing grades, adding many more extreme new routes to Glencoe. Unicorn, while an outstanding outing, is more old school and would have been a better *Hard Rock* contender than Swastika. It's all subjective though, and the books provide tales of fun and adventure on the rock.

Extreme Rock only had one print run. A fire destroyed all the typeset and so it was never reprinted. It now commands a remarkably high price among collectors of climbing books. When flat broke and fed up, wanting to walk away from climbing after another friend was killed, I sold my copy. Ed, Bernard and Janine had signed it. I got £375 for it in 2007 and put the cash towards a new racing road bike. I regret that now.

I had a big swollen ankle after Unicorn and struggled to walk for a few weeks. I didn't think it was worth going to hospital. Some years later I broke my ankle on a mountain rescue after being thrown off a 4x4 vehicle. I walked three miles to the road after that incident and Fiona insisted on taking me to hospital. On reading the X-ray of my ankle, the doctor said, "I see this isn't your first ankle fracture." I looked at the X-ray and the penny dropped that I had finished Unicorn with a slightly broken ankle, and somehow walked to the road. Ed later did an article for *Climber* magazine about our day, calling it "Curse in the Corrie".

Ed and I climbed a lot together in the early 1980s and did some new routes in Glen Nevis. He was a teacher at Lochaber High School and introduced a lot of young folk to climbing. His legacy of first ascents extends from the southwest of England to hard Lakeland routes such as Fallen Angel, Glencoe's Clearances, and at Skye's Neist Point Supercharger. His legacy are these and a host of other routes in Glen Nevis and all over Scotland. Ed was quite a character and sadly died a few years ago.

The Big Ride. Dougal Haston was born in Currie, on the outskirts of Edinburgh, and went to school at West Calder High. As a young man he climbed many new Scottish routes with Robin Smith. Routes such as the Bat on the Carn Dearg Buttress of Ben Nevis established the pair as future stars. Smith died in an accident in 1962. In 1965, shortly before his ascent of Harlin Direct on the Eiger, Haston was sentenced to 60 days in prison, having hit and killed an 18-year-old student on the old road coming from Clachaig. He was drunk and left the accident scene. Local constable Sandy Whellans arrested him.

In 1970 he and Don Whillans were the first to climb the south face of Annapurna on an expedition led by Chris Bonington, where sadly local climber Ian Clough was killed. In 1975 Haston and Doug Scott were the first pair to summit

Mount Everest by the southwest face. Haston's memorial in Currie mistakenly claims he was the first British climber to ascend the north face of the Eiger. In fact, it was done by Chris Bonington and Ian Clough in 1962. He did do the first ascent of the north face by the most direct route in 1966, with Jörg Lehne, Günther Strobel, Roland Votteler and Siegfried Hupfauer. American John Harlin was killed when a rope broke (Dougal advised thicker, stronger ropes for fixed lines). The route became the Harlin route in his memory.

Haston became director of the International School of Mountaineering at Leysin, Switzerland, in 1967, taking over from the founder, John Harlin. He died in an avalanche in January 1977 while skiing on his own above Leysin on the northeast face of La Riondaz. Strangely, in a book he had written called *Calculated Risk*, which was found after his death and published posthumously, he had included a similar end to the book's character. Quite a bit of the book is set in Glencoe and many of the characters in the book, including the main one, John Dunlop, seem to be based on real people and semi-autobiographical.

One of Dougal Haston's contributions to Scottish climbing is on the Etive Slabs. These slabs of granite are blank and featureless, and tilted at an angle where it's difficult to gain any grip or traction. Ascent is by faith, hope and friction. As they are blank, long falls, serious injury and much loss of skin can result. At 600 to 900ft long, the routes cross two distinct bedding planes where overhanging walls of 20 to 30 feet have to be got over to get onto the next raised slab. And some small overlaps. Sometimes getting over short or long traverses on the lip of the overlaps are necessary, depending on the chosen route. Falling over these can be fatal, especially if the climber has run out the rope a long way above. The hardest routes take more direct lines and that is what Haston was trying to achieve on this route. In its day it was the Etive test piece of slab ability and nerve as fall from the crux move was long, bouncy and damaging.

Haston fell off the slab many times before giving up and producing an inferior line which he called Frustration, which had a tensioned rope traverse to avoid the even steeper slab to the belay. He finally went back and straightened out the line after many attempts to give the route we know now as the Big Ride. Still graded at E3, the route requires courage and respect. I did it on the 5th of May 1983 with Wull Thomson and Mary Anne, his daughter. I still remember that day. The knack of reading the slab for tiny indents and gently rubbing off any loose grains, as the crumble of a granite grain under your rock shoe could have you falling off and destroying your confidence in the friction. The crux is at about 100 feet out with no gear, up a thin flange where the slab steepens by a few degrees. If you are incredibly careful, you can get a micro nut behind the flange before committing to the last 50 feet. That pitch is a lead of 150 feet with one poor runner, and a final 5c move takes you to the belay. A brilliant route and test of slab skill. There are many other good routes on the slabs. And Haston's test piece was later matched by a much harder and more sustained route called the Pinch Direct. Left of Big Ride is the corner of the route Agony, which is a personal favourite, if you can get it dry. This is better protected but also has some nice slab sections.

Gallows Route. First led in 1947 by John Cunningham wearing sandshoes, "Gallows" route takes a line up the right end of the east face of North Buttress. Its second ascent was by raiding Sassenach Don Whillans in 1951 under the noses of the Scots. It had rejected many suitors previously due to its boldness, as a fall from it would be catastrophic. Creag Dubh mountaineering club legend Patsy Walsh was watching unbeknown to Whillans and was so impressed he invited him into the hallowed interior of the club doss house "Jacksonville", which sits below the Buachaille. Whillans apparently said to Walsh, "Hey, Jock, where do you find these bleeding chop routes!"

John Cunningham was another of that era's legends of climbing and mountaineering, with many high-quality summer and winter ascents. He went to Everest in 1953 with Hamish on a hare-brained trip very typical of Hamish. After attending a lecture by Andre Roche about the Swiss attempt on Everest the previous year, Hamish realised that the Swiss expedition had left a series of food dumps all the way up to the South Col. Hamish thought this was too good an opportunity to miss, so he came up with the idea of a Creag Dhu Everest Expedition using the food caches. Cunningham was astonished to find the expedition was to comprise just the two of them. By the time they arrived in Nepal, the British expedition had already succeeded, making use of the Swiss food, but they didn't give up and continued to Everest Base, living on a diet of potatoes. Hamish recounted to me that even the Sherpas felt sorry for them and gave them food and cutlery.

On the day of my ascent of Gallows, I had been climbing with Wull Thomson, a seasoned mountain hardman. We had been all over the Buachaille, wandering about, doing various routes as you can on the mountain by linking up crags. We had come up from Central Buttress doing what was called Iron Cross. We then did Engineer's Crack and a route called the Widow. Then we went across and did Brevity Crack, and a couple of other HVS routes on that face. John Anderson, a local climber and rescue team member, was up taking pictures and scrambled across to us and suggested I should try Gallows route. I had not really thought of it, but hey, why not! Although quite short, the first few crux moves are about 5c and take you out on a rising traverse for about 50 feet before the first bit of protection. A fall before this would probably kill you. Gallows is a short test of bottle (courage) and thankfully I was well warmed up on the previous routes. I also had an audience of Creag Dubh climbers watching. They had come to gloat should I fall off. If I survived, I would get the piss taken for years. If I didn't, then I suspect it might only have been a brief talking point over a pint that night in the legendary climbers' bar at the side of the Kingshouse. Thankfully, I managed to climb it just fine, and so make a bit of a name for myself. And I had a pint bought for me in the Kingshouse. Getting that pint bought by a Creag Dubh club member was a greater addition to my palmarès than the route. This was in 1982, so forgive me for being chuffed, as I daresay it's regarded as an easy guidebook tick these days. After Gallows we did a route up the middle of the top tier of the crag above. Up a thin crack line well to the right of the "Hangman's" corner, and it was technically harder. Rock climbing days on the Buachaille are always special.

Carnivore. Carnivore, on the face of Creag a Bhancair, Buachaille Etive Mòr, is more commonly known as the Tunnel Wall due to its shape, as it looks like the entrance to a huge railway tunnel. The wall is perhaps 150ft high at its greatest. Using features and weaknesses for 500 feet, the route Carnivore (probably named because a peregrine falcon used to nest on its face) makes its way from the bottom left to top right of the crag. First climbed by John Cunningham and Mick Moon in 1968. A better line aesthetically was the direct finish to the route done in 1962 by Don Whillans and Derek Walker. Known as the Villain's Finish, this is the way most folk climb the route now. The original finish was no mean feat as it was very wet and often required a bit of aid. It goes free now at E3 6a.

I was beaten to climbing the route by the Villain's Finish by Fiona. George Reid, my regular climbing partner of that time, had phoned the house to see if I would take the afternoon off from cutting down trees and climb the route with him. I was away up the wood out of contact, so Fiona offered to climb it. Their back rope on the first traverse pitch jammed on them, so they climbed the entire route on a single 9mm rope. The Villain's Finish had a big reputation for being brutal, so Fiona did well on the route. To say I was pissed off I had missed the climb would be an understatement. The autumn monsoons came, and then winter, and I had to wait until spring the following year to work off my frustration and get the route climbed. I was in a hurry as it was one of the few in the graded list I still had to tick.

I press-ganged a young instructor who was a good climber working at the Glencoe outdoor centre to be my rope man that day. It was mid-March in a snowstorm. I stormed up and across the first pitch. Duncan, my belayer, linked the second two pitches into one and belayed me below the overhanging crack that gives the Villain's Finish. Good rock and hanging out over a big drop, it requires a move up and out right, with a stiff 5c pull over the bulge past an old piton left by Whillans. Then out onto the wall above. It's then a runout to the top of the crag at a steady 5a with no protection. It had started to gently snow while I was on these final gearless moves. Kev Howett and Dave Cuthbertson were on the crag that day. They had dropped a rope down much further to the crag's right and were cleaning what is now the tunnel wall bolt classic Uncertain Emotions 7b. I knew Don Whillans a bit, as he was often a Glencoe visitor. I first met him playing darts against him and Joe Brown at the Padarn pub on a trip to Wales. Passing the Villain's Peg on Carnivore that day was like passing a bit of history.

YoYo. Robin Smith and Derek Hughes climbed this magnificent route in May 1959. The line had also been tried by Don Whillans, who left his broken piton hammer hanging from a piton during an aborted earlier attempt after giving up due to wet rock. After three attempts enduring the repeated toil of a walk up past Ossian's Cave, Smith finally made it to the top of the final pitch onto the "Pleasant Terrace" (it's anything but pleasant) on a Monday, having rested the day before, a Sunday, as it was raining heavily. On the first ascent Smith spent ages drying the wet rock on the first pitch with a towel. Smith, a young, powerful climber, lost his life in the Pamirs in 1962 in a tragic accident with Wilfred Noyce. Smith was one of the very best climbers of his generation and also a very good writer. A sad loss to Scottish mountaineering. I can recommend *High Endeavours*, a tale of the life and legend of Robin Smith, by Jimmy Cruickshank as a read.

When I climbed YoYo I was recovering from an accident in the wood. As I worked as a woodcutter, accidents were sadly common. I had slipped and chainsawed my ankle and Achilles tendon area quite badly, the chain having gone through a gap between two sets of Kevlar heel pads in my boots. The tendon was only nicked, but I had unzipped the side of my leg. Lots of stitches in the Belford by a Dr Sen, and a few weeks recovery, by which time I was gagging to get a route in. Loads of holes from the stitches did not deter me from persuading Duncan Freeman, the lad I did Carnivore with, to come and do the route. On a hot July afternoon, we made our way up the scramble to the bottom of the route. That north face of Aonach Dubh intimidates me. Having been rescued off it stuck and hypothermic didn't help allay my fears. I had also taken a fall late at night in winter up there on a rescue, bashing up my legs pretty badly. The first pitch of YoYo is supposed to be hard and wet, but thankfully it was just a wee bit damp that day and fairly straightforward. The second pitch was Duncan's lead and the pitch which seemed to cause Smith problems on the first ascent. Although not technical, it was hard work, and apparently had lots of loose rock and boulders choking it on the first ascent. I found it quite hard, and it was really good led by Duncan. Bearing in mind Duncan hadn't been climbing for months, and I had been out of action for weeks, so going straight onto a hard route was maybe not the best idea. The last pitch was out into late afternoon sun on fantastic rock with the climbing exposed and 2000 feet of space below. Climbing into the sun on the steep and excellent rock, that wonderful red rhyolite, was superb and I enjoyed the lead. The route ended all too soon on the unpleasant terrace, a ledge along the top of the route. Getting off the terrace is interesting, so it was worth keeping on the rope. What a great route YoYo is. Quite thuggish but nothing too bad, and what an excellent situation and outlook. Ed Grindley's route "The Clearances" beside it is one of Glencoe's best newer routes of that time. It's a good bit harder and more serious than YoYo though.

Shibboleth. This route was Robin Smith's finest in Glencoe, and while maybe not technically the hardest route of its time, it was certainly the boldest, and it has lost none of its reputation. I know the route's history well as I knew folk that had climbed with Smith. He made several attempts at the line of the route, one resulting in a leg injury for Al Frazer, his belayer, resulting in a big impromptu rescue operation from the combined forces of Squirrels and Creag Dubh climbing clubs. Al Frazer had broken his leg badly and had to be hauled up onto North Buttress, carried along above Raven's Gully then out onto the Buachaille summit ridge, and then down to the bottom of the mountain. Smith soloed off the route to the side to go summon the help for Al, which was bold and very brave. That rescue was a huge technical and physical task.

Al Frazer later worked in Raigmore Hospital, Inverness, with a climbing friend Bill Amos. My interest in the route came from the infamous graded list in the guidebook Buachaille Etive Mòr and Glen Etive Vol 1. That guide also listed Agags Groove as a suitable route of descent from Rannoch Wall. I do not recommend that, although local climber Ian Nicholson has descended it solo. With various friends I had been working my way up the graded list and Shibboleth was second from the top. Carnivore was above it, but really Shibboleth should have been at the top as it is bolder and harder in my opinion. Many routes at the bottom of the graded list deserved a place nearer the top. The previously mentioned "sandbags". The graded list was all reputation and anecdotal, so quite subjective. Also no one liked admitting when they found routes lower down the list, which were supposedly easier, actually much harder. The top listed routes being the work of the masters of the time, no one would dare question the grade. I had looked across at Shibboleth from various angles while doing the routes on either side and watched another party from the Scottish Mountaineering Club (Graham MacDonald) on it while I was doing Bludgers/Revelation with George Reid. In the pub I had Creag Dubh climbing legend John MacLean regaling me with the tale of the second ascent of the route, which he did, and his looking for "that fucker Wheech's peg", Wheech being Smith's nickname. Hamish also told the tale of the first ascent of Bludgers route with a bespectacled Patsy Walsh, a somewhat myopic but powerful climber, and a chap nicknamed Sunshine. The route was so named as they had no food on the day of ascent and in Australian slang, a bludger is a scrounger. Now this route is linked to Revelation, giving one of the best Hard Very Severe routes in the country.

The year 1982 was a washout summer for us, and despite getting a lot of routes done in the Lakes and Derbyshire, it was a poor Scottish rock climbing season until a let up in late summer when the weather finally cleared, and we had a few dry days. On a Saturday in early September, George Reid and

I arrived at the foot of Raven's Gully and looked up at the black winking groove of the 5c second pitch of Shibboleth. By coincidence, the Scottish Mountaineering Club (SMC) party who had been on the route while we were doing Bludgers previously were back doing the same Bludgers/Revelation combo we had done when we met. Fiona gave George and me a lift up and walked up to the foot of the route to take a few pictures. She had to leave as she was guiding a group up Gearr Aonach Zig Zags later that day. I remember nervously stepping onto the first pitch, up past a block with no gear until a belay just before the winking black groove. The black groove was wet and hard with a nut hammered into the crack and an old decaying black piton. George led it with no fuss but a hint of anxiety as one foothold was black and wet and his EB rock boots were slippery. This is the technical crux and a bold, intimidating lead, especially as it's often damp in the groove. The third pitch up to below the Revelation flake was a romp of joy for me, although awkward with a sting in the tail pulling onto the belay ledge. While climbing "Raven's Edge" on Cuneiform buttress opposite with Bob Hamilton some years later, we watched Ian Nicholson take a whipper for 30 metres off this pitch when he couldn't find the crucial hold on the belay ledge as a guy was standing on it from a party in front and the ledge was buried in the ropes. Undaunted, he just climbed back up, by which time the guy had moved off the ledge and finished the pitch. He was climbing with a rope of three, the others being Wull Thomson and the famous "Human Fly", the legendary Joe Brown. Joe came up to Glencoe on a fairly regular basis through the 1980s and we locals shared a rope with him. He was everything that folk said about him as a rock climber. Strong, with quietude and grace, it was a privilege to watch him climb or share a rope with him. He was also humble and a really nice man.

The next pitch of the route is up the wall to the right of Revelation flake. A long pitch of steady successive 5a/b moves on little rough holds on a vertical wall over a huge abyss, followed by a pull over a small overhang then up the wall to the belay. With only one running belay, it certainly focuses you with the gaping maw of Great Gully and Raven's Gully winking from the shadows below. Very absorbing climbing. The final two 45m pitches to North Buttress are easy 5a climbing up steep walls. You just know you will go back one day, as most of us do, and do the route again then traverse right across the cave to do "The True Finish" which Smith added later. The *Hard Rock* book version is the 5a finishing pitches. On finishing Shibboleth that day, we went across and did Yamay E2 5b, Yam E1 5b, Happy Valley E1 5b and May Crack VS 4C alongside Tam Macaulay and Dave "Paraffin" of the Creag Dubh MC, who were climbing on the same crag. They seemed very impressed we had done Shibboleth with the crux groove so wet. We went to "The Ferry Bar" that night (under the bridge at Ballachulish Hotel), which was "the" climbers pub at that time. Ian Nicholson and several others shook our hands, saying, "well done, lads", and for the next week we had folk saying, "I hear you guys did Shibboleth, well done!" It was nice for once to feel the equal of the legends past and present. I felt like I had arrived at something and wasn't an imposter.

Mountain Accidents

Folk have been getting into trouble in the mountains for a very long time. Recreationally, mountaineering and climbing as a sport really took off in the latter part of the 19th century. Early pioneers, many of whom were the founders of the Scottish Mountaineering Club (SMC), would make their way to Glencoe via train to Bridge of Orchy on the newly completed West Highland Line then take a horse and cart to Kingshouse or, when motorised, along the improved old Glencoe Road. The upper glen and Buachaille Etive had some of the best climbing of the day, with test pieces of rock climbing such as Crowberry Ridge via the Direct route. Lower Glencoe was less accessible as the road wasn't good. Later SMC climbing meets at Glencoe Hotel were attended by members coming via the newly completed Oban branch line to Ballachulish via Connel Ferry and later the new Connel Bridge opened up the lower glen. The railway made the lower glen and Ardgour much more accessible. These mountaineering club meets also included exploratory trips to Garbh Bheinn over in Ardgour. Garbh Bheinn is a fine mountain often overlooked unjustly in favour of its higher Glencoe neighbours.

Winter mountaineering epitomises Scottish mountaineering at its best with its variety. Snow, wind, poor weather and short days. Sometimes you are rewarded after a winter ascent, when breaking out of the icy confines of a gully into the gloaming of a deep cold sunset, snow on faraway hills, pink and blushing. Then as darkness descends and you're late off the mountain, the northern skies brighten, and a sensuous, sinuous light dances its merry jig and fills you with joy.

It's an incurable affliction. Attempts to regulate our culture and recreation have left mountaineering as a last bastion of freedom where genuine adventure can be sought out, without rules and regulations. Rescuers are mountaineers and all mountaineers potential rescuers and should not be judgemental as one day it might be their turn. Of course some may become armchair pundits, risk averse and critical, but that is anathema to the spirit of mountaineering and of course mountain rescue.

You will find many tales in Scottish Mountaineering Club (SMC) Journals of tragedy, self-rescue, and local stalkers and shepherds going to the aid of the injured or dead. These fellow mountaineers or local hill folk taking the lead in forming a search and rescue party. Some notable and epic incidents have occurred in the past. A climber injured up in Arch Gully of Stob Coire nam Beith required a telegram be sent to the SMC clubrooms by his companion, requesting climbers to come and help. The club's steward was off for the weekend, so the poor casualty had to wait until the telegram was opened on his return for the extra help to get to travel to Glencoe. The rescue party of climbers, shepherds and stalkers went up with their modified wheelbarrow and carried him to safety. Other stories include the fallen climber laid to rest in the

Sunday best room off the Elliot family's cottage, with the Elliots and some rescuers waiting for the undertaker in their parlour, perhaps having a dram and cup of tea, then hearing a stramash as the casualty came round, probably warming up from hypothermia. These were the tales I heard and wished I had listened to more. As the post-WWII years progressed, so did tourism and more organised mountaineering club visits to Glencoe. The new A82, as it is now, made Glencoe a relatively easy day trip from the central belt, or as a weekend destination. Post-WWII, and in particular from the late 1950s, up to 40 incidents occurred each year requiring some form of either self-rescue using equipment based at key rescue posts such as Kingshouse, Clachaig and Achnambeith or, more often, assistance needed from the local hill men and police. It became obvious that a more formal rescue setup was needed and so Glencoe Mountain Rescue came into being.

Looking back to before the rescue team was formed, you can only admire the courage of these ad hoc rescuers, going to the hill to search or evacuate those in trouble. In the early part of this century, mountaineering was largely a middle-class pastime. It is a testament to the early rescuers that, despite seeing the early climbers as a somewhat eccentric bunch, it never deterred them in the slightest when help was required. Nor I doubt would it ever have crossed their mind not going to help someone in trouble. Often these rescuers were ill equipped, with only paraffin lamps to guide the way. These rescue parties carried out some amazing feats. Aitcheson, the farmer and stalker from Gleann Leac na Muidhe, or one of the shepherds or farmers in the area, be it from Achtriochtan or Achnambeithach, Dan Mackay at Altnafeadh or Downie from Allt na Ruigh, would cycle around to gather a search party, perhaps including the local policemen if fit enough and available. If it was an overly technical rescue, additional manpower would be sought from any climbers in the area or, as mentioned, a telegram sent to the Scottish mountaineering clubrooms for assistance.

Later, as mountaineering grew in popularity, a new class of mountaineer appeared from mountaineering clubs such as the Lomonds and the Creag Dubh. With little money and poor equipment, these clubs relied on the hospitality of Dan Mackay or Downie for a doss in their hay barns at Altnafeadh or Allt na Ruigh or stayed at a makeshift doss in an old fank at the foot of Meall a'Bhuiridh. Post-WWII some of these Lomond club members went on to provide the skier rescue when alpine skiing started at Glencoe White Corries (now called Glencoe Mountain). A weekend trip to Glencoe for the pre-WWII generation was a real test of determination. Finish work on Saturday afternoon, hitch or scrounge a lift on a passing lorry to the Glen, doss the night, climb next day then try and get back for work on Monday morning. For a taste of the adventure at this period in mountaineering history, the book *Always a Little Further* by Alastair Borthwick captures this effort and enthusiasm. Even in this little gem of a book, there is a rescue. A second could not follow his leader when exiting from the "Devil's Cauldron" of the Buachaille Etive Chasm, a classic gully climb of its era. The leader got up to the top, but his second could not follow, so he descended to the Glen Etive Road and stopped the local butcher who had been delivering meat to Glen Etive. The two of them went back to the top of the climb and pulled the stranded climber to safety, landing him "like a 12-stone salmon". The local butcher was the father of a neighbour of ours in Lorn Drive when I was young.

After the war, mountaineering took off in a big way with a proliferation of climbing clubs, mainly from the universities. This popularity resulted in an increase in the accident rate, but due to the clubs coming to the Glen as bus parties and mostly climbing in one area, there was often sufficient man and woman power available for self-help rescue. This ability to rescue themselves, and the increasing number of incidents, prompted the provision of first aid and stretchers at rescue posts in the Glen by the newly formed Mountain Rescue Committee of Scotland. Groups could get access to equipment and effect a self-rescue with a proper stretcher. Previous to this it was known for a casualty to be carried off on a stone mason's wheelbarrow or some similar improvised transport.

As the post-war years progressed, accidents became even more common due to more people taking to the hills, having more recreation time. The RAF Mountain Rescue, which was primarily for the rescue of downed aircrew, sought a new peacetime role. Many weekends would see RAF MRT in the Glen. Volunteers just like their later civilian counterparts. From RAF Kinloss, or more commonly to Glencoe, Leuchars MRT. These RAF teams conducted many rescues in the Glen, and when the civilian team was formed, they provided additional support on protracted searches or busy weekends. This working relationship was particularly close between RAF Leuchars MRT and Glencoe MRT. Later when the Search and

Rescue Wessex helicopters were based at RAF Leuchars, there was a strong working bond with aircrew and the Glencoe team.

Several figures deserve special mention in the history of mountain rescue in Glencoe: Dr Donald Duff, surgeon at the Belford Hospital, and of course Hamish MacInnes. A history, no matter how brief, would not be complete without mention of the Elliot family, who without doubt set the foundations of the early team and who continued to take part in rescues until the late 1990s. Walter Elliot senior and his sons William and Walter received a certificate for distinguished services to mountain rescue in 1976. Another potent figure from the early days pre and post formation of the rescue team was Sandy Whellans, first as a local constable and later as a sergeant in the Argyll constabulary. A strong personality and a commanding voice often heard before he was seen. Sandy took part in many difficult rescues. John Arthur of Gorteorn Farm, Ballachulish. John Anderson, Davy Todd and Dennis Barclay of Kinlochleven. The Knowles brothers, and a great stalwart of the team, Eric Moss, who came to the team after leaving the Army (Argyll and Sutherland Highlanders) in which he had retired as a major. Huan Findlay from Achtriochtan was a powerhouse on a long stretcher carry. His son also became a valued team member. Malcolm, son of team member Alan Thompson, and Jamie, the son of another long-standing team member Wull Thomson, are second generation rescuers. Many bar staff from the Clachaig Hotel took part in ad hoc rescues over the years, some going on to become full rescue team members after taking up residence in the area.

*Davy Gunn climbing on Ardverikie Wall.
(Photo by Dr John Main.)*

Fiona Ducker, soon to become Mrs Fiona Gunn, climbing Clachaig Gully. (Photo by Dr John Main.)

Fiona Gunn racing her mountain bike at 10 under the Ben bike race. (Photo by Fraser Copeland.)

Hamish MacInnes sitting on Dr Tom Patey's old Ullapool surgery chair. (Photo by Davy Gunn.)

*Davy Gunn in white helmet assisted by Andy Nelson
treating a seriously injured climber, Buachaille Etive Mor.
(Photo by Davy Gunn.)*

Wessex helicopter from RAF Leuchars. Call sign Rescue 134. Evacuating an injured climber from Sron a Creise Glencoe. (Photo by Davy Gunn.)

Fiona and Gunn family, Tignes, France. (Photo by Davy Gunn.)

*Avalanche with seven injured, Lagangarbh, Glencoe.
(Photo by Davy Gunn.)*

*Davy Gunn, Glencoe Ski Patrol Rescue Team.
(Photo by Davy Gunn.)*

Three Sisters, Glencoe. (Photo by Davy Gunn)

Davy Gunn on the way to Holyrood to receive an MBE for services to mountain rescue. (Photo by Julia McCue.)

Hamish and Mountain Rescue

The Glencoe Mountain Rescue Committee (later reformed to Team) was formed in 1961 at a meeting convened at the Clachaig Hotel, Glencoe. The meeting was called by Hamish MacInnes, then a resident climber and climbing instructor in the Glen. The committee consisted of Dr Duff, then resident general surgeon at the Belford Hospital in Fort William as president, Hamish MacInnes as secretary, Brigadier Martin as honorary president, and a Mr McLaughlin as treasurer. The Elliot family of Achnambeith were elected to the committee, although absent from the inaugural meeting. William Elliot senior had already taken part in many rescues and his two sons followed suit in the years to come. The Elliot family were a keystone of rescue in Glencoe. The small cottage in which they lived had been the focal point of many rescue operations, and it would be true to say that literally hundreds of mountaineers have received succour from the family while awaiting news of injured or lost friends. Also elected in their absence were Dennis Barclay and J.W. Simpson. Dennis became the rescue team's treasurer for the next 24 years. A thankless task in the early years. In addition to the office bearers elected at the meeting, other founder members present at the meeting were Hector Beaton of Achtriochtan Farm, J. Feeny, E. Blackhall and J. Robertson. From that inaugural meeting in 1961,

Hamish was to be the Glencoe Mountain Rescue Team leader for the next 33 years. Hamish had an engineering background and for many years was at the forefront of mountaineering both here in Scotland and abroad. Hamish was one of the great technical innovators of mountain rescue. His textbook, *The International Mountain Rescue Handbook*, was regarded as a definitive text on the subject. Hamish was instrumental in the formation of the team and, like Dr Duff before him, designed a stretcher. The "MacInnes" stretcher is still a workhorse of Scottish mountain rescue. Known by some as the Old Fox of Glencoe, Hamish lived in the Glen for over half a century. He moved into the small cottage of Allt na Ruigh, above the meeting of the Three Waters in 1959 and moved further down the Glen to the National Trust-owned Achnacon in 1973. He later built his own home at the site of an old sawmill on the old Glencoe road between the village and the Clachaig.

While doing his National Service at the age of 17, Hamish was posted to Austria. On the limestone walls of the Kaisergebirge, he acquired a taste for piton bashing from the Austrians. His attraction for pegging later earned him the nickname "MacPiton". Routes like Porcupine Wall on the Cobbler, Engineer's Crack on the Buachaille and many routes on the Skye Cuillin had the odd piton used to aid progress, as well as Titan's Wall on Carn Dearg Buttress and Ben Nevis, which is now a high-quality free climb. The ubiquitous piton was often used for aid and that's just how it was back then. They had none of the cams, nuts and modern protection available nowadays. Tied into the rope with no harness and only a bowline around their waist, falling off wasn't only painful, but could also be terminal.

Early in his climbing career, Hamish was rescued. The first incident occurred in the French Alps. Teenage Hamish had an arrangement with the well-known and famous French guide Lionel Terray (first ascent of Makalu and author of the tremendous book *Conquistadors of the Useless*). As route finding was difficult, Hamish had arranged with Terray that he would solo climb a short distance behind him and his client. On a traverse of the Grand Charmoz, the guide pair made a 40ft abseil from an in-place nylon sling over a bollard. Hamish threaded his rope and proceeded to follow suit abseiling, only for the sling to break as soon as he weighted it. On hitting a small ledge at the base, his knees were driven up to his face, temporarily blinding him. Luckily, he didn't fall down the remaining 500ft drop to the glacier below. Another famous Swiss guide, Raymond Lambert, was nearby and him and Terray rescued Hamish.

The second incident occurred during the winter of 1951 whilst trying a first winter ascent of Raven's Gully on the Buachaille Etive with Creagh Dhu members Charlie Vigano and John Cullen. Hamish was leading the climb and a long way out on the rope when the rope jammed (it was also dark by then). Unable to free it, he untied and continued upward, reaching an impasse just below the top. He bridged across the iced-up chimney and braced himself for a long night, dressed in jeans with only a thin shirt underneath his jacket. His rucksack and warm clothing were with his companions far down below. They fared much better as they were wearing heavy motor bike jackets. Fellow Creagh Dhu climbing club member Bill Smith was driving up the road and spotted the faint head torch lights and, along with others, including Jimmy Marshall (one of Scotland's best mountaineers), went up and dropped a rope down to Hamish, pulling him up to safety in the early hours of the morning. Hamish was so cold he thought he would die!

Hamish was a memorable character. If I had owned a decent camera in my early climbing and rescue years, one picture I would certainly have taken is of Hamish in Glen Etive beside an abandoned minivan. We had gallon cans of beans in our old rescue truck as sustenance, and, lacking a plate and spoon, there he was sitting on a rock beside the river with his iconic cap on, eating cold beans out of a mini headlight glass with a big dirty channel peg. That image will always stay locked into my brain as the epitome of a hardman climber. Yet behind that picture was a gentleman.

Dr Duff, who helped form Glencoe Mountain Rescue Team at that first meeting, was also instrumental in forming the Lochaber Mountain Rescue Team. He took part in many rescues on Ben Nevis and Glencoe. Dr Donald Duff, surgeon and mountain rescuer, was born in Edinburgh in 1893 and educated at the Royal High School of Edinburgh. He studied medicine at the University of Edinburgh. After graduating he joined the Royal Army Medical Corps and served at the Battle of the Somme. In 1918 he was awarded the Military Cross.

Dr Duff served in India in 1919–20. He became a fellow of the Royal College of Surgeons of Edinburgh and worked as a Senior Resident Surgeon at Craigleith Ministry of Pensions Hospital, Senior House Surgeon at Leith Hospital, House Surgeon at Salford Royal Hospital and the Surgeon at

Denbighshire Infirmary in North Wales. He worked in North Wales for 23 years and took charge of two Red Cross hospitals and the Civil Defence Medical Services during WWII where he reached the rank of lieutenant colonel. Dr Duff began his climbing in Snowdonia and took part in mountain rescues in North Wales. He also designed a stretcher that bore his name. In 1945 he became a general surgeon in the Belford Hospital, Fort William, joined the Scottish Mountaineering Club and became involved in mountain rescue as both a rescuer and surgeon, treating casualties on and off the mountains. His lightweight mountain rescue stretcher, the "Duff stretcher", became standard kit in Scottish mountain rescue until replaced by the stretcher designed by Hamish MacInnes.

Dr Duff should certainly be regarded as a father figure of mountain rescue in the Lochaber area. It was his motivation that organised the formation of the two mountain rescue teams, bringing together local shepherds, mountaineers like Hamish and other local hill men on a more formal basis. Up until this point rescuers were a hotchpotch of whoever could be got hold of at the time of an incident. A telegram would be sent to the Scottish Mountaineering Club in Glasgow for assistance or, if on Ben Nevis, assistance requested from the Lochaber branch of the Junior Mountaineering Club of Scotland when technical climbers were needed.

Early Rescues

It's very likely that if you're a competent mountaineer or climber in a poorly populated mountain area, you might decide to join a mountain rescue team. That may occur either by chance while out mountaineering and coming across an incident you help at and coming to the rescue team's notice, or through friends and acquaintances. You will be invited to come out with the rescue team on a training exercise to see if you fit in and are physically fit enough. My involvement started when I was 14 years old. I would often see my neighbour from a few doors up, Cecil MacFarlane, go out with his rescue dog, a large German Shepherd. He asked me to go out on avalanche training days with the newly formed "Search and Rescue Dog Association" also known as SARDA. They would bury me in the snow for the dogs to find.

For the next two years, I would be a pretend casualty for the dogs to dig out on the annual training weekend. From getting to know folk there and being keen, when there was a mountain rescue callout, I would just turn up and help on the rescue if I could, often in small ways like carrying the wheel of the MacInnes stretcher on its awkward mounting frame, which no one else wanted to do as it was uncomfortable.

I was not allowed to be a full member of the rescue team until I was 18 years old and could be covered by the police insurance, and when the rest of the team were confident that I was competent enough. I climbed quite a lot for a young boy. It just seemed a logical and natural thing as a mountain enthusiast to be part of the rescue team which had most of the active mountaineers in the area as its members. Some who were among the best mountaineers in the UK at the time. I perhaps hoped some of their talent would rub off on me. The jury is out on that.

My first rescues were in the early 1970s, more than a decade after the formation of Glencoe Mountain Rescue Team. To begin with there were no mobile phones for emergency calls and very, very rarely a helicopter. A typical rescue weekend at busy periods would include at least one rescue from Clachaig Gully, sometimes three. And long stretcher carries, such as on a physically hard weekend on two consecutive nights carrying badly injured climbers from the Lost Valley Buttress to the A82 roadside. There were also many big searches for people missing in the area. Often these folk were missing somewhere in Glencoe, and we had no definitive information. Without a helicopter these searches were all footwork, and often we would be out for three days or even longer. This changed for the better in the mid-1970s when RAF Leuchars had the Wessex helicopter, and we did not have to rely on the slow Westland "Whirlwind" which had to refuel several times on its way from RAF Lossiemouth. The Wessex helicopter was a game changer for mountain search and rescue.

Every rescue team member will have rescues or incidents that stayed with them and made an impact. Probably different rescues for each team member depending on their personality or skill set. Personally for me some have stayed with me because of the emotional toll they took. Rescue is a team effort, so when reading the tales that follow, please allow that these are only my perspective on the events. Some rescues will stay with all of us, as the impact was so great, or the incident so bizarre. With nearly 40 years of mountain rescue and 20 years of ski patrol alongside other things I have done, there are many incidents to choose from. Too many perhaps, so a triage of suitable tales to tell was needed. I decided some were too grim to write about or too close to home, such as when friends had lost their lives.

There were some very odd rescues over the years, such as a drug-crazed naked man on the summit of the Buachaille Etive Mòr, and the search for Mr Sparks, who was missing in Glen Etive for six very hot days. The police called the search off for Mr Sparks and the helicopter flying home flew over a deep gully for one last look. The crew spotted a small red dot and, unsure what it could be, came back to pick four of us up. We were winched down at the edge of the gully and rock climbed down the deep gully wall to see what the red thing was. After climbing down really horrible death-if-you-fall terrain, in a wee hidden corner we found what appeared to be a corpse covered in blow flies, with maggots crawling over open wounds. The corpse opened an eye and said "hello"! Looking rightward from the very much alive Mr Sparks, the team leader John was traversing in towards Andy Nelson and I and the two RAF mountain rescue lads who were with us.

John was on heather and loose rock above a 300ft drop, using a deer antler like an ice axe. Despite extensive injuries Mr Sparks survived. All week his wife, a very sanguine lady, had turned up each morning at our RV (meeting point) with a small table, a chair and a picnic, sitting and quietly observing, offering us tea from her big thermos.

An early mountain rescue recollection is turning up as an aspiring team member aged about 16 to a rescue on a rock route called "The Mappie" on Gearr Aonach where a fallen rock climber had sustained a serious spinal injury. Everything was in hand when I arrived, but a short while later there was a report of a fallen female on the north side of the Aonach Eagach. As most folk were dealing with the original call, I went around to Caolasnacon on the north side of the ridge with Sandy Whellans and a deer stalker from Dalmally. The stalker was in full estate rig, and he was also a special police constable with Argyll Police Mountain Rescue Team, who were sometimes called as backup to Glencoe Mountain Rescue. Argyll Police rescuers were based at Oban and Lochgilphead as part of "Y" Division and we knew them as the "Y Fronts".

We headed up to below the pinnacles, past a wee rock shelter with a horse's bridle in it. Local men Seamus Pharig (James Macdonald) and Peter MacNaughton of the house "Cruachan" in the village had made this wee shelter when they were employed around 1922 to set the boundary or "March" fence up onto Meall Dearg, along some of the easier bits on the crest of the Aonach Eagach ridge to Stob Coire Leith. Many of these old metal posts are still there. We found the poor woman who had fallen, dead, just above the rock shelter. This was the first mountain fatality I had been at, and it was a bit of a shock. Somehow the banter between Sandy and the stalker allayed any disturbing thoughts at the time, especially as the stalker, who was quite a colourful character, had smelt a fox and was hunting for a den nearby. The rescue team arrived, the poor woman was put in a body bag and then stretchered off down the mountain to Caolasnacon. That initiation to the cost of falling off a mountain set me to thinking about being a mountaineer, but somehow then, as later happened so many times, it gets firewalled, and you pretend to yourself that you are more able than the fallen. Utter nonsense, of course, but it worked. It's worth noting that at one point all the early Glencoe Mountain Rescue Team members were required to be special constables if they wanted to be covered by insurance. This didn't last for long, as the newly formed Mountain Rescue Committee of Scotland and local rescue teams managed to negotiate cover from the police or took out their own team insurance cover.

I remember a very long winter night on Beinn an Dothaidh above Bridge of Orchy, finally finding missing Dundonian climbers stuck below a huge cornice on what could have been the route Taxus on its first winter ascent. We roped them out. It sticks in my mind as it was a Wessex search and rescue helicopter that came to help, but it couldn't get to them. The keeper MacRae at Achaladair persuaded the crew to fly him up when the rescue was over to collect some red deer hinds he had shot the day before. Beinn an Dothaidh is now covered by Oban Mountain Rescue Team. Up until the year 2001, this was also part of Glencoe MRT's area.

A harrowing early rescue tale was searching the winter climbs of the east face of Gearr Aonach and helping recover two young female students from St Andrews University, both hanging on a rope either side of a tree after a main belay failed a few pitches up Lost Leeper Gully. At that time, the pitch in question only had a single piton belay and it was a well-known poor belay. The leader must have fallen and pulled the belayer off. Down they catapulted until snagged by the rowan tree. It was a macabre sight. It was also where I first met the legendary Mick Tighe, who was on the path below with clients he was guiding and who offered to help with the hefty stretcher carry back to the road. We only needed to get them to the floor of the valley as thankfully a helicopter managed to get in and lifted them out from the valley floor. But it was still a messy task and hard work.

In the small community of Scottish mountaineering, it's inevitable you will be called to help or pick up the remains of people you know. This happened more than I care to remember, and it was not always from great hard climbs or mountaineering feats that they lost their lives. One night walking across the bridge to the Lost Valley, I saw a glint of reflective tape up the river gorge from my torch. This is not where you expect to find a talented mountaineer. However, going in to see, I found the missing person laying there having run off the path, coming down at speed. He had fallen 20 metres down onto the rocks and slipped, dead in the water. This same person who I had seen soloing without ropes half a dozen rock climbing routes up on Rannoch Wall in a morning.

When dealing with tragic events as a rescuer, you are engrossed with the job at hand with little spare bandwidth for anything else at that time. The unsung heroes of MR are those back home, looking after family and worried. Seldom acknowledged, the family get none of the kudos of membership of the mountain rescue tribe and are left to manage. Despite whatever kudos there might for the rescuer, don't imagine it's easy getting out of a warm bed on a bad night to wander over the Aonach Eagach looking for someone. I make no bones about how anxious I was sometimes. Torn with anxiety from leaving a young family and feeling selfish. I also had occasional bouts of depression, and I was full of self-doubt. I learned to mask it. Possibly not very well. Masking mental health issues was partly because in my experience some folk weaponise it against the individual if they carry a grudge or have envy, and I did experience that, even within mountain rescue. However, friends stand by you, and that's really what teamwork is. Honesty and being supportive off the mountains as well as on. I had some good friends and colleagues, and the shared ups and downs are what build the trust that is required when tied into a rope or during difficult or stressful times.

In one early rescue with Hamish, I had been given some new boots by the rescue team. My old ones had been left in the porch at the front entrance of Kingshouse Hotel in February of that year after helping out on a winter rescue from below Raven's Gully, where very sadly a young lad had died. The casualty was 17 and so was I. Someone left me one of my size eight boots, and one of their size tens. Despite asking Jim Lees, the hotel owner and manager, to ask around, after waiting for a few months, the boot had not turned up. Sandy Whellans, the local police sergeant and rescue team member, mentioned it to Hamish, who very kindly had a pair of new ones sent up from George Fisher's climbing shop in Keswick. In between times I made do with old worn-out Galibier "Super Pro" leather boots, bald and leaky and with toe caps stuck on with Evo-Stik glue to cover holes. The new boots were Lionel Terray "Fitzroy", which, like the Galibier "Super Pro", were the winter climber and alpinist boot of choice of that time. Heavy full leather boots with a metal shank, they took a bit of breaking in. I went up the Pap of Glencoe in them one Saturday. The Pap was not a popular hike back then. It was a rite of passage for local teens getting to the top just to say they had done it, but other than that you rarely saw anyone going up. The Pap has been a good training route for me over the years, both hiking it and running it many times, once as a bet to the top and back from the church in Glencoe in an hour. I even did a winter climb up it once, on its north side on rock-hard snow and ice, up and over rock steps at about grade II/III. Such stunning views north from such a small hill surrounded by Munros.

The day for breaking in the new boots was overcast but dry. I went up and down the Pap quickly, meeting no one else on the way. You would be hard pushed to find it that quiet now, as it has become so popular. I walked back down to the village when I saw Sandy Whellans, the local police sergeant, coming toward me in his van. He stopped and suggested I jump in, as there was someone badly injured in Clachaig Gully. There are many deep gullies around Glencoe and Glen Etive. The Buachaille Chasm, Dalness Chasm and others, but Clachaig Gully was by far the most popular. "The Gully" has a lost world feel to it. Deep and mostly wet, although sometimes a heat trap in direct summer sun. Above the ascending climber, the walls hang with vegetation and loose tree-lined rock on vertical and overhanging side walls. The Gully is about 37 pitches in all, with four of real note. The Great Cave, the Ramp, Jericho Wall, and the Red Chimney. Jericho Wall and the Red Chimney are above the tree line. Jericho Wall was so named as the walls of the Gully are only five metres apart at this point. The pitch goes up the right (east) wall. Famous Scottish mountaineer W.H. Murray, the first ascensionist, likened Clachaig Gully to a "monstrous beauty like the hindquarters of an elephant", quoting Elroy Flecker, a playwright and poet. Murray's first ascent of Clachaig Gully, with Marskell, MacAlpine and Dunn, was made famous in his classic book *Mountaineering in Scotland*. I grant you that I was young for rescues, but I had already notched up a few harder climbs, had epics, been on a few rescues, and I had been rescued myself, not that that should count for anything. I thought I could handle myself, and at least I was strong.

The lower gully pitches are short and escape from the Gully confines easy, but they have nippy little technical bits for the unwary, or for those not used to climbing in boots. One pitch of note has relatively recently disappeared after rockfall. Before the collapse of that particular lower pitch, the trick was to bridge up using the gully sides and up below a short waterfall which could be dammed up with clods, and then burst to soak the second as a bit of fun. It's a short, hard, bouldery move to get over now and very different. I did it just after the rockfall and, reaching over the top, felt a latex glove which was mine from a fatal accident I attended two months earlier. The casualty on that occasion was climbing second on the rope several pitches past the Great Cave when his friend knocked off a large rock. This struck the casualty on the rucksack and hit an aluminium water bottle that broke ribs and punctured his lung, causing a condition called a pneumothorax. Even though we were very quick to get there, by the time we had been called out, run up and abseiled in, it had gone into tension, a serious and immediately life-threatening condition. Despite resuscitation efforts and advanced life support, he did not survive. Those that deal with these medical emergencies know that a lot of kit gets left around, and even though you try and tidy up, on the rocky bed of a gully, stuff gets missed, especially in the dark.

Several parties would climb the Gully of a weekend back when this tale occurred. As a result, it was well visited by the rescue team, often called there twice in a weekend and several times a year. An average roped time to climb the entire gully would be about five hours, although on one ascent for a party of four, it took two days. Hauling stuck folk out of the Gully high up in its upper reaches was a fairly common event, but also there were sadly some nasty accidents and fatalities. Back then the Gully was graded Hard Severe. It has been soloed by many, including my late wife Fiona with Cynthia Grindley one evening, but back when this story took place, I had not yet met Fiona, my future wife.

Back to this tale. I jumped in the van with Sandy, and we parked up at Clachaig where Hamish was waiting for the old green ex-Army rescue truck, our mobile rescue base, to arrive. A vintage vehicle from the UK Civil Defence, it was pre-power steering, needing double de-clutching and a strong, brave driver. Huan Findlay, a local shepherd, was bringing it from the Elliots' house where it was kept at that time. Sandy mentioned to us that someone else had also called the police very worried as they had friends doing the Aonach Eagach Ridge that should have come back down by now. We meet with the fellow who reported the Clachaig Gully accident. He had abseiled down "The Great Cave" pitch, leaving a fixed rope, and then come out via an escape route path on the west side, then come down to the hotel to phone for help. His friend had fallen off "The Ramp" pitch, the technical crux of the Gully (4b/c) and, with no running belays, had fallen about 50 feet onto the rocks on a ledge above the Great Cave.

Hamish and I set off up the path at a fast pace to find the exit point of the escape path (path might be the wrong term) and then scramble down into the gully. Hamish had some technical gear, a radio and some first aid and I had nothing. We climbed the Great Cave pitch solo. It is not a hard pitch. It goes up to a tree, then a step down, and then a move across to a short corner and up to the ledge where the casualty was lying. The poor fellow was struggling when we arrived. He had a broken jaw, broken wrist and a chest injury along with nasty scalp wounds. He was not wearing a helmet, but he was conscious and in a lot of pain, so we decided to give him some analgesia.

Opiates for chest injuries can be controversial as they can depress the respiratory drive. However, if the casualty is in so much pain they cannot move their chest wall and breathe, and there is no sign of a lung injury such as a pneumothorax, then it is a good thing to alleviate the pain. Hamish rummaged about in his wee red stuff sack with the first aid kit in it and handed me a syrette of "Omnopon", which is an opiate like morphine. I injected it into the loose skin on the back of the casualty's hand and then we bandaged him up the best we could. It was not possible to get at an arm or pinch some belly fat as injection options.

Sandy Whellans radioed Hamish to say he was organising a helicopter to look for the folk on the Aonach Eagach and maybe to help us out as well. And that a new report had come in that shouts were being heard coming from around Ossian's Cave. The helicopter was coming from 202 Squadron, then based at Lossiemouth. Getting one across to the west was quite a big deal as they need to refuel, and it is a long way for the Whirlwind, which was a wee helicopter.

The rescue truck had arrived as a base station. Rescue team members waiting below were asked to bring up a stretcher, casualty bag and a long static rope. Eventually this arrived at the gully below us and we used the climber's rope left in place to get the static line attached and pull it up to us along with a big sling to make me a harness, along with a descender device for getting down. This was for me to abseil with when the time came. Hamish spied a good strong rowan tree 15 feet above us and took an end of the long static rope up and tied it to the spindly but apparently well-rooted tree. We pulled up the stretcher and casualty bag, having also asked for another rope to be tied onto the foot end of the stretcher. The stretcher was hauled up, and between us we got the casualty onto the stretcher with a lot of humping from us and groaning and pain from him. Challenging work for just two of us, and painful despite the analgesic for the casualty. Hamish got out two swing cheek pulleys he had made in his workshop. Rustic but functional homemade pre-Petzl equipment. He also had his own design homemade rope jammers. We rigged the stretcher with tape slings, as the Mk 3/4 MacInnes stretchers didn't have wire strops pre-fitted for hoisting. We then put the pulleys on the static line and clipped them to the top and bottom stretcher tapes and connected up our climbing rope as a back rope to the stretcher on a belay. Then we got the bottom end of the static line taken up and out of the gully floor and up onto the path to the west side of the gully, where there was a group of rescuers waiting. We asked them to tension the static rope tight and lock it off on a good belay. This was more like a tug of war as five hefty rescuers hauled in the rope. The static rope was angled down at their end and was much lower than us. The rope tension lifted the stretcher airborne above us and clear of all obstacles and we could then lower it with our back rope to control it as a "skyline". Someone in the gully below grabbed the rope attached to the foot end of the stretcher which hangs below, then walked it out of the gully as well. They joined another rope onto this in case it was not long enough, pulling the stretcher as needed to coax it out onto the west side, away from Hamish and me. It went well, sky lining across the width of the gully, airborne until our rope ran out and the stretcher arrived at a good landing on the other side below and across from us. It was then carried by team members over the short distance to the path and a flatter piece of ground. A couple of hours had passed, but the timing was perfect as the weather was good and the helicopter arrived flying up to where the stretcher was waiting uplift. The "Whirlwind" only had a 60ft winch wire, so it did not have a lot of capability, and certainly would not have been able to winch the casualty from the gully below.

The "Wessex" helicopter from 137 Leuchars which replaced the "Whirlwind" a couple of years later had a 300ft winch and twin free gas turbine jet engines. It could, at a push, take up to 16 people in it (although not in its SAR role where seven-plus crew was a load). The Wessex helicopter and its RAF Leuchars aircrew changed mountain rescue for the better and without doubt saved dozens of lives, perhaps even that of the mountain rescuers, by snatching casualties from extremely dangerous cliffs and gullies where risks were high when they could and the weather was favourable.

That day the casualty was picked up by the Whirlwind and flown away to the Belford Hospital Fort William. To get down Hamish and I had to abseil off on the abandoned rope doubled and pull it down after us. We scrambled out onto the path and made our way down the steep path to the roadside. Twenty-five minutes later we were at the base vehicle to be told Sandy was up on the ridge on his own and had found the missing folk and was guiding them down. We went up the Glen with the binoculars to see if anything was visible at Ossian's Cave. Sure enough, there was a group of about seven people, and they were waving a big orange plastic survival bag. We asked for the helicopter to return, and it did so and lifted up a couple of team members, winching them down near Ossian's Cave. One casualty with a broken leg was winched up onboard quickly, and then the rest of the group guided back down to the bottom of the hill. There is a particularly good picture of the pilot that day, John Stirling, landing the helicopter on the A82 to pick up team members, the traffic stopped on either side of the road. It had been a busy day. As we were near an excellent pub, we made the most of what was left of the day, and quite a lot of the night, refreshing ourselves with beer.

Mountain Medicine

Remote medicine and first aid are critical skills for a rescuer. Some take that interest to higher levels of qualification or have a professional medical interest. I had an interest in the medical aspects of rescue and trauma care from seeing so many folk needing help. I was an early school leaver with no qualifications other than from cutting down trees and hard work. I was persuaded by Fiona that I should do some adult learning and get some qualifications. I gained qualifications in human physiology, pharmacology and eventually became one of the first UK paramedics. This was before the NHS had any paramedics, and only some RAF search and rescue winchmen had undertaken advanced life support training. I was never going to be a doctor, which had been an ambition, as leaving school early had scuppered that. I wasn't stupid it seems and Fiona, who was a very clever woman, could see that. Fiona was dyslexic and often put down as stupid. Anyone that knew her will tell you she was quite the opposite. In fact she had a very high IQ and phenomenal pattern and problem-solving skills. She was just slow at reading and handwriting. Word processing liberated her from that as it did for me, or you wouldn't be reading this!

Despite little schooling, later in life l was invited into the Royal College of Surgeons Faculty of Pre-Hospital Care as a founder member, and the British Association of Immediate Care Specialists as a full member. I would not swap these early years in the woods and the people I worked with for any degree, or the adventures life brought later. Secondary school failed me at a formative time. But perhaps it was karma, and that wasn't my path.

Hamish once said to me "Carry a camera, Davy, one day it will carry you." I was late to taking photographs. Fiona was the one most often snapping away with her Olympus OM-1 SLR. This changed when I bought a small compact film camera. Mostly I took slide pictures using Kodachrome 64 for summer climbing, and for rescues Kodak Ektachrome 400, which worked better in poor light or at night. The advent of the digital compact camera was a revolution. Gone was the excitement of waiting for a box of slides to come back, and anticipation of how many were duds. It was always worth it for the five or so really good ones from a box of 36 slides. Digital changed all that and Microsoft PowerPoint reigned supreme for lecturing. Folk have always joked at some of my injury pictures. I can assure the reader that I only ever took pictures with permission, and never at the cost of patient care. People often joked at lectures that I followed Airway, Breathing, Camera, but I can assure folk that circulation always came before camera. A camera has financially carried me, so it was good advice from Hamish, as I was able to use my own pictures when talking on the medical aspects of mountain trauma. My interest in the medical aspects of rescue came long before a camera.

As a young mountaineer and rescuer, I remember a few harrowing mountain rescues when I was often left wondering what we could do, if anything, to improve the care of those we found and evacuated. Frequently they were in acute pain, and sometimes circling the drain hole of life, where survival was at best 50/50. Some sadly didn't make it, although on reflection even with the best of modern medicine and equipment, the outcome might possibly be the same due to the severity of their injuries. We got them to hospital alive, even if only just alive, but they were too badly injured to survive. Mountain rescuers, whether medical/clinically minded or technically skilled, have to make an immediate choice at a rescue scene where someone is badly injured. Is it better and safer for the patient (and rescuer) to rescue the patient from the scene before medical interventions, or is it a critical situation for the patient, when immediate medical intervention must take place before rescue from the scene, in order to save the patient's life? I was very aware of the consequences of occult injury and a strong advocate of a team approach to lifting and managing a trauma casualty. Some of this came from the school of hard knocks to myself, as I was already a pupil.

Rescue from the accident scene, along with good basic first aid, is the default position, and one at which mountain rescuers in Scotland are very adept. Back in the early 1980s, nothing much had changed for decades in the application of basic first aid. Ambulance service staff were a transport service with limited interventions. Prehospital emergency care, as it is now known, was in its infancy. Changes in trauma care in the UK were on the way, although at first often reluctantly accepted by the establishment. These changes were based on aspects of the American Department of Transport Emergency Medical Technician and Paramedic programmes for prehospital care. *Emergency Care on the Streets* by Nancy Caroline was the bible of emergency care at that time, and the American Advanced Trauma Life Support course for accident and emergency doctors was just gaining a foothold in the UK.

In the 1980s I was already trained as far as I could go in first aid. I was then fortunate to be invited onto the first Scottish and second UK ATLS course. Advanced Trauma Life Support is a structured approach to managing trauma. I had done some college courses and gained qualifications in human physiology and pharmacology to help with background knowledge to be a paramedic. Next stage was Advanced Cardiac Care, including paediatric care and a course with BASICS, the British Association of Immediate Care Specialists. After some clinical placements, at that time requiring intubations and at least 40 emergency cannulations, I became a registered paramedic, of which there were probably only half a dozen in the UK at that time. Later came the Health Professions Council (HPC), which I successfully registered with as a paramedic. The public mistakenly attribute being a paramedic to all providers of emergency care, but in fact it is a protected title and those that use it are trained beyond the level of technician. It's not easy to get registered. It's illegal to call yourself a paramedic if not registered with the HPC.

The structured and algorithmic ATLS approach to treating immediate life threats, reducing pain and reducing complications from hidden injuries following a systematic and proactive approach to managing and immobilising a patient, was a simple but effective algorithm to apply under stress. Perhaps we could reduce mortality (deaths) and morbidity (long-term consequences) in the mountains by following this structured approach? The challenge was applying it in a hostile mountain environment safely for both casualty and rescuer. There should be only benefits to the patient with no time delay in rescue, or rescue safety compromise beyond that already acceptable to a group of skilled mountain and ski rescuers.

Taking this approach required other rescue team members coming on board and acting much like the core group of practitioners you will see at any major trauma call in accident and emergency departments. A team working simultaneously on various aspects of care. In addition on mountain rescue, aspects of physical rescue from the scene such as belays, ropes, etc. need taken care of. It's an integrated approach. The rescue team leader takes overall control of the rescue big picture, leaving the rescue medical providers to treat the patient. A team approach and medical oversight by the most experienced team medic on scene. Not unlike an A&E trauma call, but without monitors and scanners, only snow, ice or rock and perhaps turning rotors and a maelstrom from a helicopter overhead. I must pay tribute to Hamish MacInnes for supporting this approach. John Grieve became leader after Hamish retired, at a time when there was a big increase in mountain rescues in Glencoe. In particular there were many more casualties with life-threatening trauma. Patient-centred care with John leading and coordinating some very difficult rescues, leaving me to manage the patients.

It should never be forgotten that mountain rescue is a team business, and leadership medically is but one aspect. Management of the rescue in general is equally as vital so things are done safely and in a timely manner. There were times when objective dangers nearly changed the outcome, but it's a risky business being on a mountain, and luck is required. I like to think the team approach to casualties might have made the difference for a few poor souls.

Many of the Glencoe team's first aiders became advanced first aiders by taking the Ski Patrol Emergency Medical Technician training, of which I will discuss more later. These colleagues were very adept at managing a patient well, with my skills not always or rarely needed. One skill I had which I used often was to give intravenous pain relief with strong opiates or similar medications. Sticking a needle or "cannulation" into a cold, frightened and distressed patient was a skill I was quite good at and gladly so, for many casualties went from high pain scores to comfortable while enduring long, tortuous evacuations over rough ground, or down long climbing routes.

I had a range of resuscitation equipment and analgesia to bring to the casualties. While I could and did intubate (inserting a tube down through the vocal cords), most poor souls were too far gone. Close attention to maintaining the patient's airway and delivering oxygen were crucial to all injured patients. I believe that basic first aid done well is better than advanced care done badly, especially in a hostile environment. I had the first ever defibrillator in Scottish mountain rescue, delivered in 1990 from Marquette via RL Dolby of Dunblane. Some ridicule ensued with comments like "All you will give the patient is a curly hairdo" from the legendary Mick Tigh. Mick was Scottish Mountain Rescue training officer. I was Scottish Mountain Rescue training coordinator for a couple of years before him. A strong mountaineer and rescuer, I respected his opinion, but not over defibrillators. In fairness he came round in time.

Within a year the defib was in action several times, and on one occasion a Laerdal FR 1 defib, which replaced the heavy Marquette, delivered 27 shocks to a patient before her heart restarted, although sadly she did not survive to hospital discharge. Traumatic cardiac arrest and hypothermia the cause in this case. The casualty fell into the river at the Lost Valley bridge.

Another aspect of taking medical care to the mountains was finding medical equipment that was up to the job. The kit for immobilising fractures had not changed much for decades. Some rescue teams still had a "Thomas" splint (developed in WWI for midshaft femur fractures where its use dramatically reduced mortality, but it was difficult to apply on a mountain). With prehospital care developing as a speciality, there was a rethink and redesign of kit, especially in the USA. Quite a lot of early prehospital medicine was also influenced by military practice. Some of these practices were harmful in the long run, so we had to be circumspect. The prehospital treatment of blood loss shock up a mountain was simple for us. It was to plug all the wounds you could see externally by looking at the patient's back, front, left and right (expose, examine and reveal), apply large wound dressings or a coagulation dressing, then evacuate in a helicopter as fast as possible to the staff waiting to receive the casualty at the hospital. The hospital being updated by mobile phone or via the police. The A&E and surgical team were ready to go to theatre and stem any blood loss internally from spleen or liver tears or insert chest drains. Geoff Lachlan, Dave Sedgwick, Brian Tregaskis and the Belford staff were great support on and off the mountains. Dr David Syme, then medical officer to the Scottish Mountain Rescue Committee, was tremendous in supporting trials of new kit, with a view to making suitable equipment available to all the teams if worthy. I am also grateful for the tremendous support from within ski patrol, especially from the medical officer Dr Ian MacLaren, consultant in A&E at Monklands Hospital, and the late Dr John Scott, London HEMS, who both encouraged and trained me over the years. In particular, though, "the Doc" Ian Maclaren, who provided support and was always there at the end of the phone for a debrief after a difficult resuscitation.

One vital bit of kit I was pleased to introduce to mountain rescue was the American "Hartwell" Vacuum Mattress. Before the vacuum matt we had no way of effectively immobilising people with a spinal injury. Spinal injuries are devastating. Using the matt, which wraps around and encases the casualty, helps prevent movement, reduces pain and provides insulation.

We also introduced extrication collars which, when used appropriately, are a way of stabilising a neck injury until the casualty is safely in a vacuum matt and supported. I am sure this saved many people from life-changing consequences. We also had Level One Trauma Splints sent across from the USA, with some of these excellent splints still in use many years later. Other notable imports were a good casualty bag from

Colorado to keep the casualty warm, and the first reliable pulse oximeter from the company "Nellcor". Oximetry is a useful tool in the context of other vital sign checks.

From 1992 Tony Cardwell of Nevis Range Ski Patrol and I, through BASP (the British Association of Ski Patrollers), started the Ski Patrol Emergency Medical Technician Course. For 14 years Tony and I took turns as course directors. We had the course endorsed by the Royal College of Surgeons (Edinburgh) to give it a bit of clout, and for many years pre mountain rescue "Cas Care", it was the go-to course for advanced first aid medical training for Scottish mountain rescue and ski patrol. These EMTs were the backbone of medical provision in Scottish MR for a long time. We followed the "train hard – fight easy" concept as espoused by the military. These were stressful training courses with practical medical and trauma tests to pass, and an exam to finish. After six days and nights of morning lectures, outside scenarios up a mountain or down by a foaming river gorge in the dark, students were better equipped mentally to provide care in a hostile environment. We had special forces medics and expedition leaders come on our courses as well as mountain rescuers and ski patrol from all over the UK. Over the years many memorable incidents occurred on these courses, one in particular at Glencoe Outdoor Centre on a night exercise down at the sea pool below the centre with the river rising and a spring tide. The tide came in around the scenarios in the dark and not until Tony Cardwell put up a flare did we realise we were cut off. Carrying the volunteer casualties out at shoulder height on MacInnes Mk 6 stretchers in vacuum matts in the rising water, with the rescuers up to their waists in it, proved a realistic and memorable night. On another occasion I had the entire course flown by Sea King up to a simulated crag rescue up in Glencoe where one of the volunteer casualties was the Squadron Leader at 202 Squadron, the base for search and rescue helicopters. In the wind and rain, this crag rescue was as realistic as you could get. Training hard builds spare thinking capacity, preventing cognitive and physical overload. In real emergencies some of the tasks required to be completed while stressed are done unconsciously from this repeated practice freeing up capacity. Spare thinking time and physical reserves free up the rescuer to deal with unexpected demands and decisions. Only by scenario-based training that is realistic and stressful can this be achieved. A few tales of actual rescues follow, where training hard certainly helped.

Some Mountain Rescue Tales

North Buttress in winter. North Buttress was the second major rock climb on the Buachaille, climbed in 1895. And it is also a wonderful winter climb, full of interest following a line of shallow chimneys with a long final wander up the buttress on easier ground to the summit.

It was a Saturday evening in February and John, the team leader, had received a call from the police that a climber had taken a lead fall on the third or fourth pitch of the route, sustaining a spinal injury. I was already at the Kingshouse Hotel that evening when the radio call came over, as I was giving a lecture on mountain trauma to a group of doctors having a conference at the hotel. I made my apologies and, as I had gear in my car, changed and headed down to our RV point. One of the rescue trucks was already there, driven up by Andy Nelson, so we grabbed some kit and headed up the mountain. We soloed up the route, which was in very good icy winter condition. As other team members arrived via radio, we sorted out a rough plan.

A group of strong rescuers led by Arthur Paul made their way to the top of the mountain with two 250m ropes and gear in order to descend towards us from the upper reaches of the buttress. On reaching the casualty and his friend, Andy and I found things were a bit tight for space on the icy ledges and our options a bit limited. After my examination of the casualty, he seemed neurologically intact, although he had bits of bony spinal process sticking out of his back from a gaping open wound. It was clear to us that physical rescue from the scene was the only option. Eventually the end of a long 250m static rope snaked down to us with a second long static line also tied to it. Our belays were not good enough for a lower, so Andy would lower me and the casualty down the chimneys, and the other line going up to the top would function as a backup belay, and if required, it could also be attached to get me down if my rope was too short.

Andy had the onerous task of managing this skein of icy rope. I made up what is known as a "Y" hang and got the casualty between my legs. To survive, the casualty has to help, so I got him to use his hands to help me negotiate the twists and turns of the chimneys as we were lowered down the narrow icy slot. It was hard physical work and there was a lot of pulling, pushing and cajoling, and a hint of some fear looking up an 11mm polyamide rope thread snaking 500 metres up the buttress. Eventually I saw the lights of rescue colleagues below. They had a stretcher, vacuum matt and casualty bag sitting laid out and ready for the casualty at the bottom of the slot. I was able to get the casualty straight onto the stretcher where he was untied and packaged up. Andy tied off the 250m rope and abseiled down. Arthur and the lads pulled the other rope up and began the tricky navigation back off the mountain. It was their home patch and they knew it well. They had icy ropes plus all the technical gear, which is heavy, getting on for 25kg for the rope alone, never mind personal kit and the hardware. These guys were strong, capable mountaineers.

We were fortunate as a rescue helicopter had been tasked to come see if it could help us after completing a rescue task on Ben Nevis. Just as it came into the Glen, there was a slight lull in the wind and snow, and it was able to come in and winch the casualty away to hospital. Sometime in the night, when we were all home in bed, the temperature went up and it thawed. Next day Andy decided to solo back up North Buttress in the rain and slush to collect the rope he abseiled off on and left the previous night. Such is the dedication and technical skill of some Glencoe team members. Andy has since become an IFMGA guide and is current leader of Glencoe Mountain Rescue Team.

Willie and the light. It was late January. Fiona and I had moved from a tied Forestry house in Achindarroch, Duror, to Glencoe the previous year. That winter I was still working a forestry winch with a felling team. It was a good winter, with hard, cold conditions, and I had already been out climbing. About 7.50pm in the evening, our phone rang. It was Willie Elliot phoning from Achnambeith, wondering if I fancied a wee walk up the path which begins across the A82 from his house, the path that comes down from the Aonach Eagach. He could see a faint light high up. He told me that the light was very dim, and that he had seen other brighter lights moving about earlier. He thought it was likely to be a dropped head torch running out of battery. However, it was bothering him as he thought he saw it move just a little bit, although he couldn't be sure. "Have a wee walk up, Davy, and take a radio and let me know when you have it and are back down, okay." Fiona ran me to the end of the old road in the car and I wandered up. Willie had just put out a radio call to say I was on my way up to have a look. Team member Pete Harrop said he would come up behind me to keep me company. As is often the case, team members fancying some exercise also decided to come along for the social, and Wull Thomson said he would wander up later too.

Guided by Willie on the radio, I walked up the steep path with Pete not far behind. I was aiming for where the normal descent path goes right and there is a prominent gully on the left (west), with a small side branch forming a waterfall which Willie and Walter call "The V". The shepherds often have their own local descriptions of features they use as markers for the gathering of sheep. I still couldn't see the light, so Willie guided me in by radio to above the waterfall and then up into the snow-filled gully. The snow was hard but took a boot edge. A mountaineer died in an avalanche in this gully in the late 1950s, and the Elliots helped on the recovery of the fatality.

After about 45 minutes up the path, then climbing 300 feet up the gully, I found the light. It was attached to the head of a young boy of about 12 who had got himself in a bivy bag, wrapped up to keep warm. Not at all what I had expected! A quick chat and physical exam revealed that both of the boy's lower legs were broken. He was very worried about his dad, who was higher up the gully. Pete was a minute away and I called on the radio for a full team callout, and I also got some more information from the lad. His dad prepared him well should anything ever happen on their adventures, and he informed me he had done everything his dad told him to do. Get spare clothes on, get wrapped in a bivy bag, put a light on and flash it. Only the flashing of the light was missed out, and to be fair the head torch he had was failing and dim. No LED lights and long-lasting Duracell batteries at that time. His dad was in front of him descending the gully when he slipped and lost control, going out of sight down the gully. The young lad tried to follow his dad, then he too slipped and fell. He remembered passing his dad in the gully and told me his dad was bleeding and asked if I could quickly go help him. The lad was stoical and, considering his injuries, did not complain of much pain, although he must have been experiencing a lot. A brave lad indeed.

The snow gully above is about winter grade II and there is a short, steep pitch. I put on my Chouinard rigid crampons, which were not that long off my feet from climbing earlier in the day, and I prepared to go up. Being fit enough for a climbing day and then a night out rescuing is all part and parcel of being fit enough to be in Glencoe MR. I left Pete with the boy. Pete is a real gent, and the right guy at the right time as he had a calm, soothing manner talking to the lad and reassuring him while waiting for the rest of the team to arrive.

Wull was coming up behind me, having passed Pete and the boy. After about 200 feet I found his father, who had sadly succumbed to his many injuries and was stuck in a steep narrowing of the gully. That the young lad had fallen the same distance then even further and flown over the top of his dad and survived is something of a miracle.

Wull and I came down to help package the lad and wait for a second stretcher and more manpower so we could go back up and retrieve his father. Despite a bit of difficulty, we got the poor man in a bag on the stretcher, then lowered him down and out to the side of the gully and then onto the descent path. We could go a bit faster than the front party who had the lad, who by now was in some pain and receiving Entonox, an analgesic gas. Their journey down required much more care. The lad went off to the Belford Hospital by ambulance, and his poor dad away with the police to Glen Nevis mortuary. Later when I told Willie, he was quite visibly moved by the young lad's plight and his courage. In my experience Willie was not a man that easily showed emotion. Willie's intervention and intuition saved the boy's life. Had he not seen the light and got curious, then the outcome would have been very different. Both Willie and Walter Elliot had saved many lives, not only directly on the hill, but also with their keen eye and sense of when something isn't right. It could be a car parked for a bit longer than normal, a light high up, or talking to us rescuers by radio and guiding us along the sides of the Aonach Eagach or Aonach Dubh in the dark, following faint sheep tracks going into places where sheep and humans alike would get stuck.

We all went home with our own thoughts after the rescue that night, and as best we could, we buried the emotions of this rescue among the detritus of previous rescues. I learned later that night that the boy's family lived in Taynuilt, which is a fairly small local community not far from Glencoe.

A few weeks had passed, then I received a letter from the lad's mum to thank the team for its work that night. She gave a special thanks to Willie, who had written her a beautiful letter saying how proud she should be of her son and his courage. And how proud his dad would be of how he conducted himself, despite the pain and everything he endured that night. She was very moved by this letter from Willie and emphasised how much it had meant to her. That Willie wrote to her has always stuck with me. He could be a man of few words, but when he spoke they were worth listening to for sure. I believe she also wrote back to him to thank him for writing his kind words. I am not sure she realised it was Willie that saved her son's life.

Maybe this is just another rescue tale, but it reminds me that I was fortunate to be a part of a group of folk where empathy and compassion were of equal value to technical ability, and that casualties were not just a statistic. I am sure this is still true today, although it is a great shame that shepherds and stalkers, the true mountain men hefted to their glens, are fewer in number now.

Carnage on Central Grooves. It was a summer day and most of the climbing stars of Glencoe Mountain Rescue were away in the Swiss Alps with Hamish "The Old Fox" MacInnes. The team guys out in the Alps were doing safety cover on a big film project called *Five Days One Summer* starring Sean Connery and Betsy Brantley. Betsy was the performance model for "Jessica Rabbit" in the 1988 film *Who Framed Roger Rabbit*. For the film in Switzerland, she played Kate, who falls for the mountain guide taking Connery and her climbing.

Many of the Glencoe MR team working on the film were the same folk from the Glen who worked with Hamish on *The Eiger Sanction*. At the time of this tale, Ian Nicholson and Dave Bathgate, two Scottish climbing legends, had recently bought the Kingshouse Hotel, a famous mountaineering base. Lochaber Mountain Rescue stalwart Willie Anderson was painting walls in exchange for beer at the hotel. The hotel was old and needed a bit of work. Wille would not go short of beer.

The house phone rang at about 2pm on a nice sunny August day. "It's Doris Elliot here, Davy. There is a rescue call out on Stob Coire nan Lochan for a fallen climber. I can't get many of the team on the callout list as many are away." Doris would phone around and call out the rescue team. She was Walter and Willie Elliot's sister and also living at Achnambeith. She had difficulty getting any of the team to answer as folk were obviously busy or away. I asked her to keep trying while I got some technical and medical gear together. A police Range Rover pulled up outside my house not long after her call and tooted its siren. Stewart Obree, one of the local constables, was there to offer me a lift to a place where a helicopter can land up the Glen. The landing area was a big parking area mid-glen where each summer a travelling family would stay in their van. The dad would be in full Highland regalia busking, and the mother and daughter selling white heather from a wee table for cash. Stewart had already requested a helicopter, and Search and Rescue 134, a Wessex from RAF Leuchars, was on its way.

We arrived at the layby, where I got information from a witness that someone was hanging free on a rope halfway up the cliff and that the woman holding the rope was screaming. I get news that the main rescue vehicle had been picked up and Richard Grieve and Hughie MacNicoll were on their way. Hughie owned "Mountain Technology", a company that made ice axes. Ian Nicholson wasn't at the Kingshouse as he was away with Hamish, but Willie Anderson, a member of Lochaber MRT, was coming down from the Kingshouse to help. We had enough rescuers to do the job, but only just. We sorted out 100m ropes and technical kit. The helicopter had landed, and the crew agreed to take three of us up the mountain to fly over the scene.

We lifted off, slowly gaining height over Aonach Dubh, circled the corrie and saw the climber was hanging via a single rope from a running belay 20 metres above him. He was two pitches up "Central Grooves" (Very Severe 4c or 5.9). He was hanging upside down just below his belayer and about two metres out, free hanging in space. It's at least a 40m lead fall. Judging by the roll of the harness down off his pelvis and the fact that he was upside down and not moving, it didn't look good for him or easy for us. With a high fall factor and hitting the cliff with no helmet, the consequences could be devastating. The woman belaying the casualty appeared to be held by a single anchor behind a single block of rock which, as it transpired, was loose and precarious.

The aircrew and I talked over the radio, and we hatched a plan. Drop Richard, Willie and I on the top of the buttress from where they would lower me down the route to make the belayer safe and get her out of the rope system for the SAR crew to winch up. Then I would get the fallen climber lowered to the bottom of the climb. While we were doing rope tricks, the helicopter would pick up any extra rescuers and take them up to hike to the foot of the climb with a stretcher, then take the fallen climber down to a good helicopter landing pickup point at the Lochan in the corrie below.

Good belays were sorted and with the difficult task of managing the unwieldy static ropes, Willie and Richard lowered me down into the top of the corner and the loose broken ground where there were rocks stacked on each other like toffee buttons, then a further 60 or so metres. I had to stop and make my own temporary belay as they had to join on another rope to get me down. This was done fairly quickly. Loose rock is a major hazard, and lots of rock debris flew past me. The wisdom of this lower was questionable, but I was committed. A few climbs up and down to get the rope directional and stop pulling rocks onto me were needed, so it wasn't a quick job or safe. *If you want safe, join a different mountain rescue team* went through my head at one point. Some of the rocks were paving-slab-sized and I was under no illusions, having been hit by one on an earlier occasion in the corner of Unicorn when Ed had pulled one off and I just escaped with my life.

On the way down the route, I saw a watch caught by its strap in a small bucket hold in the vertical corner which the climber's hand must have slid from. I saw that the single running belay he had was an old rock peg and pretty rotten, but it had held. The climber's rope was a single 9mm rope stretched so tight it looked like boot cord. I arrived at the belay and the very upset young woman, who had the belay rope which was almost at its end in a belay plate. She was held onto the cliff by a single large wire nut which she was holding in place by pushing the block back as it had come loose. I had to spend a lot of time searching out and clearing cracks for rock pegs to hold her and make a single releasable point so the helicopter winchman could cut her free without endangering the aircraft, when she was safely in the winch strop. Separately I had to isolate the active rope going to the fallen climber and anchor it.

As it turned out, I knew the fallen climber, as he ran a local climbing instruction and guiding business. The young woman was on a rock climbing course with him. The fallen climber was dead, and it was messy. I got her safe and rigged for release. I had his rope isolated and anchored so moved down to him and made another belay for me to clip into with an adjustable sling. There was a hammered-in nut on thick blue tape, which was in good condition, just where I needed it. I don't know who left it, but thank you, whoever you are. I came off the lowering rope, leaned out and hooked the fallen climber's rope with my hammer spike, and pulled him in. I put a sling on him at the chest and to his harness to level him out and attached the long static lowering rope. Then holding his rope against the rock face, I bashed it with my peg hammer. One hard blow was all it took. He got lowered about 60 metres to the foot of the corner where rescuers and a couple of coopted climbers had come to help. They got him off the rope and the body bagged, and I got the rope pulled back up to me and was lowered down to the bottom and got clear of the corner. Sounds easy. None of it was. Rockfall, an upset belayer who is at risk, the casualty's trauma and the hard physical work takes its toll.

The helicopter came in at a hover and, ever so slowly, got closer to the corner, dropping the winchman down and inching into the cliff. The winchman got to the young woman and put her in the winch strop, cut my big sling that was anchored to some pegs, and took her up. Very impressive close mountain flying and crag rescue by the winchman. She got flown down to the base. Thankfully they came back up the mountain and took us all back down to our landing area. It felt surreal as there were cars and tourists blocking the valley road and dozens of people, some with binoculars, who had been watching the whole rescue. Meanwhile the piper skirled away his plaintive notes and took his coin.

Police statements were taken. The casualty was being paid as a guide, so an accident inquiry (FAI) was likely. Chats and a brew then down to Hamish's barn to sort out kit and home for the usual ponder at another person you know being killed in the mountains. Also thinking over many "what the fuck" moments on the rescue, and what I might do differently another time. And many other rescues and lowers were to come for me in the years that followed. It takes days to come down from the adrenaline and get rescues like that out of your head. Often the best thing is to go climbing next day. So that's what I did. With a hangover.

As a postscript, Dennis Barclay, the Glencoe rescue team's treasurer, gave me a roasting for buying seven new rock pegs and half a dozen slings to replace what I had left in the rock on the rescue. I bought them from the recently opened "Glencoe Guides and Gear", a shop run by Paul and Ros Moore. I charged it to the mountain rescue account. As the team didn't have much money, he wasn't sure if there was enough in the bank to cover it. How things have changed in Scottish mountain rescue, which is now better funded. I often ponder that rescue was about climbers helping climbers, and even had these items not been replaced (sometimes they couldn't be due to no team funds), the job would get done regardless. There was a fatal accident inquiry, and the Chief Constable of Highland Police put me up for a bravery award, which I respectfully declined. The local constable being quick off the mark, good rope handling from the team above, and the skill level of the aircrew and additional help from climbers abandoning their day to lend assistance made it all work. Climbing is about the community of the mountains, and mountain rescue is just another part of looking after your own.

A near miss in No 6. Normally a fun grade IV water ice climb when lean, No 6 Gully was well banked out with snow on this February day. Perhaps grade III with a short, easy angled entry pitch, followed by a couple of smaller icy pitches and then the final steep pitch of hopefully thick snow ice. Paul Mills, a local climber, suggested we do the route old-fashioned-style by step cutting, only taking a single rope. No 6 Gully is an easily accessible route that you can do in the morning as main course, pop down to Clachaig for a pie, and then go up and do the Screen grade IV for afters. If you want a starter, then "Chaos Chimney", the slot to the right, can have a nice water ice pitch. We were in no great hurry that day as it wouldn't take long, so with crampons, a walking axe each, a 9.5mm x 45m rope and a lift from Fiona, we set off to do it. The first pitch was easy enough to crampon up, a bit of post holing up the snow between pitches, and then quite quickly we were below the almost final pitch. There is a more direct finish above or you can just exit up a short chimney right to get off and down the old fence or go around into the corrie and add another longer climb on Stob Coire nam Beith.

I led up the final pitch. Instead of keeping left and being near a corner that used to have an old piton in it, I went across and up right as it was easier to stay in balance without the need to cut so many holds. After a bit I moved back left towards the normal route. I was trying to follow the natural features of the ice and find the easiest angle. I had a sling around an ice column at the midpoint. The climbing was not very steep, and I was always in balance, with enough features to hold on to and no need to chop steps.

On reaching the top, just below where there used to be a nest of pitons on the left as a belay, I felt very uneasy. On looking at the slope just above me and seeing the amount of snow blown in around the exit fan, I wasn't happy. From above this point a climber can usually go easily up to the terrace on the left and down into No 4 Gully to climb "Christmas Couloir", or take a direct finish straight up on ice, or more commonly via a short chimney out right. Then it's an easy descent back down an old iron fence line to the path, or the lower part of Dinner Time Buttress. I had a gut feeling of unease on seeing that exit slope. It was clearly already loaded with wind slab and was continuing to load from the open slopes off Stob Coire nan Lochan above. The lower gully was not so affected.

I shouted down to Paul that I was not happy and climbing down. I left a "Snarg" ice peg and then back climbed down to an unhappy Paul, as effectively I had completed the pitch, but he had not had a chance. I persuaded him that the top slope was not safe as it didn't feel right. We back climbed down the gully to its foot. There we met a group of four other climbers, one of whom at that time was the boyfriend of a rescue team member's daughter. They had come down from Kingshouse. They asked about the conditions to which I said okay mostly, but that I wasn't happy with the final slope, so we had come back down. Paul commented that "The old boy here wimped out on the last bit." I felt I had a bit, as it was only a short plod if I had pulled over and gone up to the rocks.

We went to the road and on the way met Willie Elliot at the cottage. He called Fiona to come and collect us. Later that evening I found out that all four topped out onto that final slope and unroped. Moving up to easy ground, it had avalanched, taking them over that final pitch and hundreds of feet down the gully onto the lower slopes. This was thankfully banked out with deep snow (sometimes there is a deep hole there). Very battered and bruised, they were all surprisingly okay. The girlfriend's dad asked why I didn't warn them. I didn't feel like saying to them that it was just my gut instinct that had turned me back. That gut instinct is spatial awareness, an unconscious taking in and analysing of knowledge and subtle alerts to your senses. It's worth listening to that inner voice. It's not infallible, but most of the time it tells you something. Many years after this near miss, I read Steve Peters' excellent book *The Chimp Paradox*, which is useful in understanding both how we process information and our primate survival instincts. Famous mountaineer Reinhold Messner also alludes to this in his excellent extreme climbing book from 1974, *The Seventh Grade*.

That area, the west face of Aonach Dubh, like most of the lower altitude winter climbs, has suffered from the recent winters, being relatively frost-free at valley level. It's such a shame, as there are many very good winter climbs on the face. No 5 Gully, right of "F" Buttress, and "The Needle's Eye" rarely see a visit even in a good winter. The direct entry to No 5 Gully, "Elliots Downfall", is now rarely complete. No 4 Gully in its lower reaches is rarely if ever climbable now, but after doing No 6 Gully, it's still possible to follow a ledge east down off "F" Buttress into the icefall start of "Christmas Couloir". "Christmas Couloir" goes up past "The Amphitheatre". It loads up with blowing snow before exiting the final slope and can pose a considerable avalanche risk. Further east comes "E" Buttress with its soaring summer classic rock climbs of Big Top, Trapeze and Hee Haw. Then comes "Amphitheatre Scoop" as a winter climb with its ice column tucked away in a chimney. And if you are lucky enough to find the conditions, it has a long, steep direct start on water ice, saving you from climbing up and going along the ledge above. The gully between "C" and "D" or "CD Scoop" starts from the middle ledge and can be quite a good ice climb. No 3 Gully is a shallow, indefinite gully but has a good short ice route called "The Smear", which forms on the wall of "C" Buttress. Next comes the obvious ice smear of "The Screen", one of Glencoe's classic ice routes. One evening during January of 1979, we splinted the broken leg of author Joe Simpson and stretchered him down after he had fallen off it. Joe had the epic of *Touching the Void* fame a few years later. Across the face comes No 2 Gully with some modern mixed routes up its buttress, then "Dinner Time Buttress", named by early Scottish Mountaineering Club pioneers who used it as a quick way down for the club dinner at Glencoe or Clachaig Hotels. No 1 Gully is on the east side and of no significance as a winter climb. However, the final chimney of Dinner Time can be a bit of fun when snowed up. The final fan of No 2 Gully is used as an exit for going into Coire nan Lochan and can load up with snow, so some care is needed in certain avalanche conditions. The descent of Dinner Time Buttress is a bit of a knee-wrecker but, certainly for the competent, a good way down if you pick your way.

A Glasgow trip. I began working at a specialist Mountain Training Centre in the late 1990s. At that time I felt I was climbing the best I had done in years and I was ticking off hard climbs, racing my bike, and hill running. I had also just finished the British Association of Immediate Care Pre-Hospital Life Support course in Glasgow, and an NHS Advanced Life Support course at Crosshouse Hospital. I was still deputy leader of Glencoe Mountain Rescue, working with John Grieve as team leader. My first work at the specialist training centre was on a Sunday evening, meeting and greeting new students, briefing them and giving them any kit they needed. It was after a memorable and manic day that I turned up for my new job. Earlier that day we had a rescue training meet at the recently completed Mountain Rescue Centre which visitors will see at the village entrance. Helicopter Rescue 137, a Sea King, arrived to find us almost ready for action. Wet suits and other apparel were donned by John, the team leader, who had a cunning training plan with a stunt in mind. We landed in the Sea King among the alder-clad brush above Kinlochleven, near the WWI prisoner of war camp. It was a scene that would do justice to the classic Vietnam helicopter book *Chickenhawk*. Paul Moores, a local guide, was to climb into the gorge and simulate a broken neck. Rudimentary belays sprung up all around as a variety of instructors, guides and prawn fishermen tried to assert who was best with ropes. The result was functional and safe rather than aesthetically pleasing. Paul was packaged in a vacuum mattress, which is a whole-body splint, and a stretcher made ready to carry him up to the bank when a shout was heard. John fell backward over a 20ft raging waterfall and disappeared off downstream.

John later reappeared, wondering why nobody went to his aid, as this was his stunt to add some spice into the exercise. Most folk did not notice or were too busy carrying Paul. Much hauling and cursing and Paul was transported to a clearing in the wood and all 15 of us piled back into SAR 137 for the flight back to our base and coffee. My teammates and I disembarked and went across into the Rescue Centre. The helicopter remained parked in the field opposite the centre, rotors turning. The winchman ran back across to us as they "had a job" and needed two rescue team members plus "the medic", which was me. Ronnie Rodger, Paul Moores and I climbed aboard with no idea where we might end up. No word had come in yet from ARCCK, the rescue coordination centre, as to where the job actually was. We climbed aboard and flew southward over the now wet and grey hills. Word came over the radio that the casualty was in a serious condition after a long fall from the south peak of the Cobbler. We flew up through the mist to a ridge and saw people waving frantically. The helicopter landed on the ridge, and we got out and ran along the ridge and were directed to the casualty, who was lying at the base of a big rock face where a few people were gathered.

The casualty was on a grassy ledge 80 feet below where he fell off. He was injured and needed to go to hospital quickly. He seemed to be with a group of medical students and was surrounded by junior doctors and nurses from the hillwalking group. They were quite assertive in the company of us aliens from the sky, and diagnoses abound. As a peace-making gesture the oldest-looking of the group was given an IV cannula to put in. This he did with gusto, but he seemed perplexed as no blood came out the end, and it became clear that unlike the cannula, he was not the sharpest tool. To be honest, up a mountain doing stuff like this is much harder than doing it in a well-lit hospital department.

The casualty was quickly packaged in the vacuum matt we had, and the helicopter stretcher with him in it was then carried down a little way until the helicopter could come in and winch him up. After this the helicopter landed again on the ridge, and after a sprint back up, we got on board, winging our way to the Southern General Hospital in Glasgow, which has since been replaced by the Queen Elizabeth Hospital.

After a 15-minute flight we landed on what appeared to be a car park miles from the A&E entrance to the hospital. The winchman and I disembarked with the casualty into the back of a flat-bedded van with two porters on board, who both appeared to be chewing gum. I was met with "Ah like yer truss, Jimmy – musta been some party," referring to my ultramodern Petzl harness and various items of jangling climbing gear. After a short journey we entered A&E, and I did our patient handover. We found out later that the casualty had spinal injuries, as well as a pneumothorax and pelvic fractures. It was a good bit of teamwork between aircrew and rescuers, so we felt chuffed we had got him to care.

Sometime later in the afternoon, I came across Ronnie wandering the hospital corridors. "How's it going, Dave?" he asked. "I've been wandering around for ages." We found out that the helicopter had gone to wait on us at Glasgow airport with Paul on board. I saw a clock that and it was 5pm. I started at the centre at 7pm, so it looked like a bad start in my career as a civilian and honorary soldier at Joint Services Mountain Training. After a few phone calls to the other duty staff member Henry Methold and the police, the police agreed to take us to the airport. They eventually arrived and drove us at speed through the Sunday football traffic of an old firm match to the Glasgow airport police station. I could now make a reverse charge call to Fiona from a kiosk to say I may be late for tea. "Where the ***k did you say you are?" she said incredulously. They would not allow us onto the airfield to look for the chopper unless we got searched. So, off we went with all the dangly jingly bits through security.

We eventually got ushered to a small departure lounge and met up with the aircrew. It seemed that despite having a big yellow helicopter with RAF on the side, and flying suits and helmets etc., they also had to be searched, and they were not amused by this. Off we went to try and find what was a big ***k-off helicopter in Glencoe, but which looked like a wee budgie when we eventually found it among some parked-up 747s. We got on board and gained permission to taxi out among the winged giants. We took off into the gathering gloom and flew west down Loch Lomond. After 50 minutes of juddering and shivering, we landed back in Glencoe. After a sprint home to change, and a quick shave, I set off to start my new job. I was in the door at the centre at 7pm exactly. First student in was most unimpressed by the gloomy weather, and a bit ratty. His first words to me: "Fuckin' hell, mate, must be boring staying in this place."

I worked at the Mountain Training Centre for 15 years. The centre was part of a consolidation of the three adventure training schemes under one umbrella organisation. Its purpose was to train to instructor level anyone who would be leading groups doing adventure training anywhere in the world. Canoeing, white-water kayaking, alpine ski touring, Nordic skiing, summer and winter mountaineering and technical rock, snow and ice climbing, and caving. There are centres in each of the UK countries as well as an alpine centre in Bavaria and Nordic centres in Norway. Each of the UK centres specialise in what its locality has to offer, and for Scotland it is winter mountaineering and climbing to a high level of competency. Instructor qualifications could be via two pathways: civilian national governing body or military equivalent awards. Civilian instructors were employed as civil servant CIOs, civilian instructional orderlies. Often these are IFMGA guides, aspirant guides, mountaineering instructors or mountain leaders. The attrition rate from injury and especially overuse injury to knees was very high among staff. Carrying big rucksacks (in military speak a rucksack is called a "Bergen") wears out joints. Aside from kitting out local and international expeditions such as alpine trips and Himalayan expeditions, I had the chance to be a part of a nurturing mountaineering environment that was supportive of my mountain rescue involvement, which could also benefit from my medical skill, and use my local knowledge and climbing skills such as they are. Unique opportunities abounded for foreign travel and mountaineering if folk were of a mind to take the opportunities. I helped a few centre folk who needed medical attention or rescue from a difficult situation. I also gained more qualifications, and in an environment where many staff and students were physical training instructors, I had to be strong enough not to be just another "fekin' civvy". I held my end up well, I think. It was a great team to be a part of. I'm not sure they ever got that I didn't like orders, and when ordered would be cussed and do the opposite. That caused a few problems! Most of my colleagues from my time there became lifelong friends, so I couldn't have been too rebellious.

Down Swastika. On a hot sultry day, the telephone rang. Fort William police were calling to tell me a climber had come down and phoned 999 from a kiosk at the post office in Glen Etive. They were reporting shouts for help were coming from the Etive Slabs and a climber had fallen. Could I call out the rescue team. The Etive Slabs of Beinn Trilleachan are a stunning sweep of clean, tilted Starav granite on 40-plus-degree bedding planes. There is no glacial polish and very few holds on the steep stepped slabs of clean rock, so ascent is very much by friction. It requires boldness and commitment to complete the harder routes where long falls may be the penalty of a slip. There are significant overlaps to cross perpendicular to the slab bedding plane. Some require wild moves and some thrutching to surmount. Gear to protect you from a long fall is sparse, and once over an overlap, then another long, relatively unprotected runout often follows. Some of the western routes finish on very steep headwalls with vertical corners, and these final pitches are better protected. The meeting place for climbers at the start of many climbs is the aptly named "Coffin Stone", which is a flat and social place to gear up.

There are many fantastic routes on the Slabs, and most are about 200 metres, five or six pitches in length. It's a venue the more technically able local climbers like me know well, having done almost all the climbs there.

We got the team rescue vehicles from Glencoe police station, which was our base at that time, and we drove down the Glen. A SAR helicopter had been requested. We arrived at the bottom of Glen Etive at the old pier and parked up. There we met the police and the witness who called in the incident. A climber was hanging on a rope at the top of a climb called "Swastika". The SAR helicopter crew called me on the radio, giving an ETA of ten minutes, so we decided to wait for uplift to get to the scene. The pilot was an old SAR friend, Adrian "Hands", flying Rescue 177, a Sea King from RNAS Gannet Prestwick. They overflew the climb and decided it was not possible to put down their winchman as it was too close into the rocks. Also there were quite a few parties still climbing nearby, or bailing (retreating in climber speak) off nearby routes after seeing or hearing the climber fall.

I talked with Adrian. We planned to get the first lift with three of us up to the top of Swastika, taking long static ropes, medical kit and technical gear. Then a second lift to the bottom of the route with a stretcher. Steve Kennedy, Malcom Thompson and I got flown up to the top and were winched a long way down onto the steep slope above the Swastika Headwall. Belays were rigged and then I was lowered down the 40m corner to the climber, whose helmetless body was lying on the slab below. He was dead from head and chest injuries and hanging on a tied-off rope, his belayer having tied it off and escaped solo around difficult ground to the right of the corner, and then down the horrible difficult path to raise the alarm.

The fallen climber had done the hardest bit of the corner and was well up the steep slope above when he fell. Perhaps loose rock or ropes jammed. It resulted in a long fall with no gear over the headwall. There was just no way to get the casualty up. As we had two 150m static ropes (static ropes are non-stretch ropes, whereas climbing ropes are dynamic, so they stretch to absorb fall impacts), the plan was to lower me, with the casualty slung beneath me, down the sweep of slabs to the bottom. I thought I should be able to keep off the steepest part of the main Swastika overlap, known as "The Moustache" (it once had a few tufts of grass). The Moustache had a broom handle hammered in at the midpoint way back, now long gone. The broom handle was desperate protection to hang a sling over as the climber traversed the Moustache lip for 25 metres, pondering the enormous fall over the overlap and down the slab below. It's now possible to protect this traverse with camming devices and no need for broom handles, but a fall would still be a disaster.

We had good radio contact with each other, and the lads lowered me and my cargo slowly down on the tenuous looking 11mm static rope. Two ropes in parallel would have been safer and preferable, but more rope to manage and more people involved on technical terrain. It was a risk, but that's reality, not like a rigging for rescue training course in a controlled environment. Reality meets theory head on. As it worked out, I just couldn't get to the side, and I was committed to plopping over the 5m overhanging drop of the Moustache with my dead cargo. I was not happy about this, as the rope would have the double load and be at a 70-degree angle over the edge for the remaining 60 metres to the bottom. I tried to pad out the edge with a rope tube, but as the rope was a bowstring, I couldn't get under it. Over we plopped and down we went. It was smelly, bloody and unpleasant, but that's just the way it is. You get the job done and think about that stuff later. The lads at the bottom had a stretcher and body bag ready, so I lowered right over it and dropped my cargo. The lowering team had done a tremendous job, including tying another rope on to extend the lower to about 250 metres. They dropped the longest rope, which we coiled. The overlap had taken its toll on the rope over that edge and it was knackered. Although not completely worn through, it was badly frayed. The rope was a unique plaited static line that Hamish had ordered many years before, as opposed to the kernmantle static lines used now. I coiled up the huge length of stiff rope, then I called up Adrian on the radio and he picked us all up as a stick, including the dead body, by doing a short, fast, low hover winch. Malcolm and Steve got back up to the top of the slabs with their gear, and also got lifted out later. As I ducked past the pilot's window at the front of the aircraft, Adrian put his hand out the window, asked to shake my hand and said, "Job well done." Quite an accolade, although it was really the lowering party that were the brains. I was just the brawn. Working with 200-plus metres of rope in difficult terrain, getting good belays and lowering me in control, as well as joining ropes, is real skill. It's not everyone I would have trusted with that task. It was teamwork and managing risk in a difficult environment. We learned later that the fallen casualty was a talented researcher at the forefront of a medical breakthrough. We rescuers concentrate on the job at hand, but none of us forget that it's also some family's loss as well as a loss to society which we have been involved in.

North by Northwest. It was late February, bitterly cold and moonlit to the point of making a head torch largely redundant. Alan Thomson, a very experienced local climber, had set off earlier that day with local lad Calum MacLellan. Their route was Northwest Gully, Stob Coire nam Beith. Northwest Gully is a modest guidebook 450m grade II/III, winding its narrow way up past "The Pyramid" and "Sphinx" rock features on the biggest face in Glencoe on Stob Coire nam Beith. This face has an alpine feel due to its scale. The route, if taken direct, can be harder on steep ice, and a few climbers have been stuck on it by getting a bit lost or being slow and becoming benighted. The rock architecture is truly fantastic, and although the route is 450 metres in the guidebooks, it's actually a bit longer than that to the summit where the route really ends. That day the snow was bulletproof neve and in great condition. There were no mobile phones back then, and it was no great shakes to be back a little late. Alan's wife Anne was not too concerned when he wasn't home by five o'clock, although it was more usual for him, like me, to be back around four o'clock. When the pair had not come back by eight o'clock, Anne phoned Hamish. He wasn't at all concerned as Alan was an experienced mountaineer and Hamish thought there was no point in calling the team out when the pair were probably just finishing late. Anne, however, felt something wasn't right and she called Hamish back again later, only to get the same response. Meantime, she called me and asked what she should do. I said I would get a couple of the lads from next door, and we would go up and have a look. I radioed the team and also let Anne know that four of us were going up for a nosey, to put her mind at rest. My neighbours at that time were Peter (Chalky) White on one side and Paul Mills not far away on the other. Chalky was a forecaster with the avalanche information service, ex-RAF Rescue and a very good mountaineer. Paul "Millsy" was working as an independent Mountaineering Instructor after leaving Glenmore Lodge. Paul was staying in a wee damp hovel of a cottage next to Tigh Dearg. Alan's son Malcolm, one of the fittest lads in the rescue team, came along too as he was obviously worried about his dad.

We set off up into the corrie, moving fast, as it was now about ten o'clock at night. We made our way around the right of the corrie to the "Rognon", a raised feature on the west side up towards Hidden Gully, and we started shouting "Alan". We soon heard faint shouts coming back to us. We asked, "Is someone injured?" and could just make out that one of them was. This immediately changed the situation, and we moved into rescue mode. I called up the team and asked for a rescue helicopter. Millsy and I headed down towards "The Gate", a landmark feature in the corrie, and started soloing up Summit Gully, crossing over into NW Gully at a little shoulder. By this time, it was getting on for midnight. We climbed up steep neve and snow ice until we reached the right fork of NW Gully where there is variation finish and where we thought the pair were, given we couldn't see any lights in the more visible normal route. Chalky was able to direct our lights towards the shouts and a faint beam of light he was able to see occasionally after moving up the corrie.

The right fork goes up the Sphynx, then to the Mummy where there is an ice pitch up to the shoulder where we thought they were. This is probably old-fashioned grade IV, short and steep, and a bit of a sting in the tail after such a long climb. We got to just below their belay at about midnight when SAR 137, a Sea King, arrived in the hover 200 feet above us. It was horrendous from the downdraught, blowing spindrift down on us and bitterly cold. Alan's leg and ankle were very badly broken and the tibial plateau in pieces, the tibia an open fracture sticking out of Alan's knee after his fall. Crampons catching in a fall make horrible twisting fractures. The young belayer Calum was hypothermic and going down from the cold. The helicopter stayed in the hover above us for about 30 interminable minutes, as it was a highly technical winching operation from difficult ground. Paul and I were powerless and just had to suck up the maelstrom.

Rescue team member John Grieve could be seen in the door of the helicopter, looking down on us being deluged and buffeted and was ready to be winched down if he was needed. The winchman did a fantastic snatch rescue courtesy of a knife to cut some slings, aided by the incredible steady hover of the airframe by the pilot. I am sure Alan and Calum felt that immediate relief we all feel when lifted from fear, cold and impending doom. That moment when you get pulled into the warm red light of the helicopter cabin at night and think you might just get through this thing and see family again. Taken from terror to safety by a thin wire disappearing into a vortex. Alan spent a lot of his sojourn that night waiting for rescue, cheering up the young lad and keeping him positive. Considering his injuries and pain, quite remarkable thoughtfulness. They might both have died that night if out any longer.

Paul and I were left in the gully smothered by spindrift and frozen, facing a climb back down of 400-plus metres. We decided we were too cold for abseiling and ropes and, had we been warmer, would have perhaps gone up to the summit. The fastest way was down. The gully below had loaded up with slab to a depth of about 40 centimetres or more from the aircraft hovering and a funnel effect down from the summit slope fan, so we had to be very careful as this blown snow was onto a hard snow base and therefore weakly bonded. It's a complicated area, but I knew it as well as anyone, so we back climbed down, trying to avoid the steeper section of NW

Gully above Isis Buttress. I knew a shortcut down a narrow corridor right of Isis to descend. I remember going down first into the gully facing in, both axes placed, and hearing and feeling a whump and roar as it avalanched below my feet. I had to climb over the 30cm crown wall with Paul following. We didn't give it much thought – this stuff happens. You don't sign up for MR in Glencoe if you want an easy time. If I am to be honest, I often enjoyed the unexpected mountaineering challenge and unpredictable nature of mountain rescue, especially in technical terrain.

We continued down into the corrie where we met Chalky and Malcolm and, in the wee small hours as dawn was coming up, descended back down the path to the Elliots'. The Elliot family were all in bed, the rest of the team had gone home long ago, and we felt a bit of a letdown with no welcome, tea or medals. There was nothing for it but to go home for a brief sleep. At that time I was back up the hill to ski patrol at Glencoe Mountain for the winter to deal with broken skiers.

Calling out a rescue team when experienced mountaineers are late back is a dilemma often occurring in mountain rescue. No one wants to embarrass them by calling out the rescue team too hastily. When is the right time to worry and act? There are no right answers, and I have put my own wife in that position when late back from a new route. However, I think for Alan it was a bit too close a call and were it not for his wife's instincts and his resilience, the consequences could have been tragic. Alan is tough, but he needed a long rehab after surgery at Raigmore Hospital in Inverness.

I was very late one night, and Fiona called John, the team leader, and he rightly said we would be fine as I was with Arthur Paul and Andy Nelson, and we couldn't all be dead! Tongue in cheek and John's way of allaying fears. He was right. John had good keen instincts and saved many lives by taking no chances and getting the team out early on many future occasions when he was leader. Hamish made a call that night with Alan, and we as our brother's keeper made one too. Rescuers and mountaineers are one and the same, and God help mountain rescue if it ever loses that ethos. There is no right and wrong, and such is the burden of a rescue team leader's role. The public are probably unaware of the massive responsibility. As deputy and leader I also had to make such decisions in the years that followed. Sometimes a degree of serendipity is involved as well as judgement.

Skiing

Skiing was part of our love of being in the mountains in winter. Fiona was technically a better skier than me and had a neat, smooth, effortless carving style of skiing. We were both ski instructors, although Fiona was more qualified as it was part of her outdoor career path before having children. We were adventurous skiers. We were also avalanche naive. How we got away with some things we skied off piste amazes me now. We were Scottish skiers, having learned up at Glencoe when it was a bit more rustic and run by Phillip Rankin, who started up the chairlift company "White Corries". There was no pisting then. Wet crud, crust, almost powder and spring corn. Adaptability was key, as were good quads and knees. The skis were long and had little shape compared to modern carving skis. Generally, everyone who was any good would wear race boots and giant slalom racing skis. Using the style of the time, knees locked and bent. I guess we skied alright, and even in powder could make nice turns, for a bit.

When we first met, Fiona's family had moved the Summer Isles Adventure Centre from the island of Tanera Mòr down to Carnoch House in Glencoe. The owner of the White Corries ski school at that time was Ronnie Weir, and he was giving it up. The outdoor centre took the ski school and ski hire business over from him. White Corries at that time was mainly a weekend ski area, with special opening midweek for big groups or club bookings. It was open to the public for long holiday periods such as Christmas and New Year, two weeks during February mid-term school holidays, and two weeks at Easter. The staff were mainly locals working there as second jobs, or schoolboys. Most of the lift staff, apart from the engineer Willie Gordon, couldn't ski but soon learned. Often self-taught. T Bar jumping was the way up to the top for a lifty, and bum-sliding on waterproofs was the main way down. Or ending up on a stretcher injured if it went out of control.

Ski rescue at busy periods was by a gang of great characters. Mainly Lomond Mountaineering Club members, or hill men who had been skiing up at Glencoe before there were any lifts. They had a doss at the bottom of the hill and carried out some amazing recoveries and rescues. Modern safety bindings had not been invented when they started. Boot top lower leg fractures were a common occurrence due to the nature of the boots and the bindings. In time, the children of these early ski rescuers took up the rescue mantle and continued the ski rescue tradition up at White Corries. And they built a much better doss. The hut they built is known as "The Hilton". This is still in use and the long tradition of ski rescue continues, with a new generation of ski rescuers or "Patrollers" as they are now called. The early skiers on the mountain were mountaineers turned skiers, some of them from Creag Dubh Mountaineering Club. As lifts were installed, more of the public took up skiing and these folks were purely skiers with less of a mountaineering background. And some might say they were less hardy.

During Phillip Rankin's time as owner manager, it was the outdoor centre ski instructors who carried out the ski rescue when the weekend rescue team were not up. Fiona was often involved. The ski school and hire were located up on the plateau next to where the current café is. Glencoe has tremendous nursery areas on the plateau, and it is a good place to learn to ski. There were no drag lifts across the plateau, and only "Effie", a service lift, crossed the plateau for food, engineering spares and fuel. Effie was so named because it was effing unreliable. Beginners learning to ski had to work hard, snow ploughing down then side-stepping back up a slope. Knackering, but once up and running the delights of "The Cliff Hanger" chairlift awaited. They could sit down on the chairlift, then ski off or pile up in a heap at its terminus and then make their way down the aptly named "Mugs Alley". They were now becoming Scottish skiers and on track to skiing anything snowy in all weathers.

Although Fiona and I were very much hardy Scottish skiers, we fortunately also had opportunities to ski a lot in the French and Swiss alps through Fiona's parents, who had connections there. We enjoyed long holidays at the chalets of their friends. We skied in places like Evolène, Château-d'Oex and Rougemont in the Gstaad valley, Mürren, or the Verbier circuit and La Tzoumaz from Nendaz. We got ourselves into some scrapes adventuring. I remember one night above Rougemont. Fiona and Roger Clair, a ski instructor friend from the Glencoe Ski School, had dropped into the couloir off La Videmanette to ski direct down to the chalet. Fiona's dad and I found a different line down and even that was difficult through the trees. Her dad and I were back for a couple of hours and there was no sign of them, so we walked back up the trail to see if we could find them. We found them clambering out of the trees in the dark after an absolutely epic descent down an icy gully.

On a more serious occasion skiing in Verbier, we dropped into a very steep couloir (a gully) thinking, as we ski the Glencoe Fly Paper, the steepest piste in Scotland, this couldn't be too bad. It was 1000 feet of hard snow ice, and there was no going back up after we had dropped into it. The cable car above us stopped and people, possibly the ski patrol, watched as we side-slipped to above a narrowing and steeper section in the couloir. A fall would be down 500 feet of the remaining gully, and several more hundreds of feet down the 30-degree slope at the exit. Fiona was below, and she jump turned three times and was over the worst. I could tell she was really scared and in tears. Then it was my turn, knowing if I blew it, I would take her out as well. Thankfully, I made it. We skied down to the cable car station below and got some praise and a round of applause, then a bollocking from lift staff.

On another trip off the top of Chassoure at 2740 metres, a group of us skied back to Nendaz, going off piste down the Vallon d'Arbi, then cutting across to Prarion. It was deep snow and needed great care. It wasn't until the following day we learned that there had been another party behind us, who had been avalanched and three had been buried and not survived. Back then we had no shovels, probes or avalanche transceivers. The culture of companion rescue had not yet begun to take hold in off-piste skiing. We were not as avalanche-aware back then. I think we had mountain instincts leading to better route choices, although decisions were made mainly to save effort, and for better skiing, not for safety. Perhaps it's all luck. I can certainly reflect that experience is for sure only a sum of near misses. To survive you need to analyse them, as one day your luck may run out. I very often wonder how or why I am still here, and why others are not.

On realising this avalanche naivety, from then on I developed a keen understanding that if I didn't wise up, I was going to die young. Even despite increased knowledge and awareness, you can get caught out one day, as we humans fall into cognitive thinking traps and forget that nothing is certain in the mountains and that inevitably with enough time and exposure, we will get caught out. We are human and make these cognitive errors. If we get a kick out of skiing off piste, then our risk exposure inevitably means one day something will happen. The trick is to realise this early, try to lower your risk appetite, make better decisions and know that even if you can only alter the risk a little, by having the correct equipment such as shovel, probe and transceiver and procedures for companion rescue, you can change the consequences.

In the last few years, I have run avalanche awareness and search and rescue courses for skiers. I became an instructor for Recco, an additional detection system to companion rescue used by rescue teams. Recco is a small passive diode sewn into outdoor clothing that a Recco detector carried by a rescue service can locate. The detector is either handheld, in a helicopter or carried by a drone. In the alpine nations, routinely deployed Recco detection for searchable casualties and quickly deployed avalanche dogs increase the chance of survival.

Nothing substitutes having the three essentials of transceiver, shovel and probe and companions being slick with deploying them effectively and managing the avalanche scene well. Buried casualty survival all comes down to practice by your companions before the real deal occurs. From the time of burial, avalanche search statistics show that companion rescue gives the best chance of survival if the casualty is found and has a clear airway in approximately 15 minutes.

Scottish mountaineers do not have the same philosophy about companion rescue as today's off-piste skiers and ski tourers. The focus in mountaineering is very much on prevention, with initiatives such as "Be avalanche aware" education programmes. These are all well and good, but sadly mountaineers still get avalanched and mountaineering avalanche casualties cannot be found in a timely manner by companions, or by organised rescue, even if on the scene quickly. The rescuers have few means of finding a casualty other than probing with a long, thin aluminium or carbon fibre probe until it hits something that feels like a human. Or with luck they may have a search dog. Recco is not a panacea for this, but every year lives are saved by it when casualties are found alive, or it shortens search time, reducing rescuer exposure to further avalanches.

The fewest live recoveries in avalanches are from formal probe lines. Probe lines have found folk alive but on very rare occasions, and while most casualties are eventually recovered by a probe strike, it's down to the sheer numbers of searchers and length of time poking in the snow, mostly at the wrong end of the survival probability curve, when casualties have died.

Spot probing, a random poke in the snow in likely locations, also occasionally results in the survival of a casualty, but that is down to sheer luck, often in a small, confined avalanche. If you are searchable, you are found more quickly and more likely to survive. Deploying all these search methods at once in an organised way if the resources are available gives the better outcome.

Although I have written mainly about Glencoe and life here, I mention these alpine adventures to set the context of some of what I have written about avalanches. Scotland, and particularly Glencoe, is possibly a more hazardous place during winter than some places in the higher European Alps. Glencoe has steep headwalls at the top of valleys, and they are often the easiest way onto the ridgelines. This exposes winter mountaineers to avalanches on ascent or descent. Climbers in some of the easier gullies find the exits open out into fans that load with snow. Snowfalls may not be alpine in depth, but they usually come with wind and massive quantities of snow moving about. During blizzards snow crystal structure is destroyed, creating dense slabs of snow sometimes lying on weaker underlayers. The Scottish snowpack can vary so much within one winter season. In the Alps, above 2300 metres the snowpack remains consistent in its stability, or instability, for longer periods of time. Above 2500 metres instabilities in the snow structure can remain for a whole season. In Scotland's maritime climate the snowpack can change in just a few hours. During the winters of 2009 and 2013, the snowpack varied greatly, and in March of these years, there were buried weak snow crystals called "facets". Then it snowed heavily on top of this weak layer. This type of snowpack is more alpine than Scottish. The buried weak layer was not obvious, not being on the surface, and was just waiting on a trigger. On two occasions the trigger was an off-piste skier. In the winter of 2009, two were injured in Glencoe, and in 2013 one well-known Glencoe skier was killed. Both incidents occurred in exactly the same place with similar snow structure events and weather patterns. Alan Dennis, an expert avalanche forecaster working in Canada, Chile, New Zealand and Scotland and author of the book *Snow Nomads*, often spent winters working for the Scottish Avalanche Information Service as he was fascinated by the variety of a Scottish winter season. I recommend his book to anyone wanting to understand the vagaries of avalanche forecasting and avalanche control.

Avalanches and Head Games

Avalanches have always been a stressful thing to experience or to rescue casualties from. Looking back, I can see how this began to affect me over time. It really began to take its toll from the harsh winters of 1993/94. Hamish had just retired as Glencoe Mountain Rescue Team leader. The new rescue team leader was John Grieve, an experienced local mountaineer and mountain rescue veteran. I was deputy leader and team medic. The previous winter, and then the summer leading into autumn, was very busy for rescues, and as autumn came early at the end of September that year, the mountains already had heavy snowfalls. In October we were called to a helicopter crash involving aircrew from a helicopter operation based in Inverness. This involved people that many of us knew very well, having worked with them on films for Glencoe Productions, Hamish MacInnes's film company. The helicopter had a cargo hook strike on the hill called Sgorr a'Choise above Ballachulish village while putting out salt blocks for sheep nutrition. I will not easily forget finding a pair of legs sticking out of the peaty hillside caught in my torchlight. Later that autumn snow came in hard and deep from an Arctic blast and two climbers were buried by snow after a fall from Northwest Gully, Stob Coire nam Beith. Both were five metres down when located by probe search, having fallen and slid, roped together, into a terrain trap well down below the gullies. In this case it was two 3m steel probes joined together to reach the bottom of the snow and a remarkable find by an RAF mountain rescue colleague helping us. Two weeks after this rescue, we were out looking for a missing winter hillwalker, and after a four-day search we found the young man dead in an icy gully after a bizarre series of events involving a "medium". The medium that a team member consulted turned out to be correct on the location, which surprised many of us. And it surprised him, having walked directly to the area she had picked out. All we knew was the missing person had gone to the summit of the ski mountain, having talked to staff on his way, saying his intentions were to walk the Blackmount hills. That night a full winter storm set in for two days and we had a missing walker, deep snow and a huge search area. I am sceptical of mediums but confess to being quite spooked by that day and how it all went. Some of that perhaps from the macabre nature of the scene and the casualty's position. Dealing with death, gore and bodies, you can become inured to. But that does not mean a loss of respect for the casualty and empathy for families. Sometimes it's not the unpleasantness of the task at hand that can get to you. The place, the light, the position of the casualty and the circumstances can get to you.

After this came the Christmas and New Year "come up and get me" from flashing lights and folk benighted or stuck, followed by severe winter blizzards in the new year leading to extended road closures from massive drifting. During this time I was working as the solo ski rescuer/patroller at Glencoe

Mountain on weekdays, and often rescuing skiers by day and climbers by night. On top of that my sleep was often broken with two young children at home. Esther, my daughter, and newly arrived Duncan.

John Grieve was the leader of the team from 1993. A mountaineer with an intimate knowledge of Glencoe, John had strong gut instincts which would ring alarm bells if we were alerted to someone missing or late off a mountain. In February 1994 John came on the team's radio (team members all have radios on at home for getting called out with a telephone backup), saying a small family group of three had walked up into the entrance of the access corrie to the Buachaille and not returned.

The wife and mother of the missing walkers was at the Kingshouse Hotel. John told me things just didn't feel right to him, so believe me, you stop eating your tea and take notice when you hear that. The preceding days the corrie headwall had been loading with windblown snow, although some climbers had taken a chance and come down it. As it's not too difficult going up into the corrie to below the headwall, we thought and hoped the missing folks were just stuck in the dark. However, from the get-go it felt like it wasn't going to be good. Just an uneasy gut feeling you get. There is something you feel sometimes in the mountains. A precognition, as subconsciously your brain is adding up observations and information. Perhaps this is a legacy from our evolution as Homo sapiens, what the author Daniel Kahneman labels "system one" in his seminal book, *Thinking, Fast and Slow*. Fast, intuitive, associative, metaphorical, automatic and impressionistic. It operates without a sense of intentional control, always active, and can't be switched off. A legacy survival instinct.

Perhaps emotionally intelligent people are more open to these precognitive thoughts. Unconsciously making safer decisions, more reliable gut instincts. Perhaps you can take the person out of the Stone Age, but not the Stone Age out of the person. Ask any lifelong winter mountaineer about gut feeling and backing off, or if they have ignored it and gone onto an avalanche-prone slope. They will tell you they just knew they had blown it seconds before the "whumpf" noise of slab avalanche release. If lucky, they get to back out and survive.

The headwall loaded with snow, the time since they left the roadside, no lights, no signs and a cold stillness. Both John and I knew this wasn't going to be good. A group of us left as a fast search party, including Steve Kennedy, Pete Harrop and Malcolm Thomson, who were in the lead with me, and Hughie MacNicoll, Wull Thomson and Kenny Lindsay and his search dog further back. It had become noticeably warmer since the initial callout. From minus temperatures to above freezing and light snow and sleet. Team members were strung out well behind as they waited on us reporting what we found. We went up into the gulch, a terrain trap feature about a third of the way up the corrie, where we went in among big broken wind slab avalanche debris, working our way up to a little re-entrant frozen stream that comes down from the "Dwindle Wall" side of the corrie on the west. I was all for getting stuck in and starting a spot probe search.

Steve stopped and said he was not happy, and I remember saying "Come on, lads, let's just get stuck in" when Steve said "listen" and then shouted "avalanche!" I hadn't heard or seen anything, but folk were scrabbling up the rocks out of the gully and I rapidly followed. At first it didn't seem real. The hiss from a big, wet monster avalanche was flowing past and around us, and up the sides of the gulch, like a super-fast snow tide lapping at our feet as we scrambled up. It was very scary and all happening very fast. Steve's gut feeling seconds before undoubtedly saved the lives of about seven Glencoe MRT that night. The gulch was now full to the brim of deep, wet snow on top of the earlier debris pile. Impossibly deep to search, as perhaps now 15 metres deeper than when we went in. Shaken and overwhelmed by the depth of snow the missing casualties might be buried in, we abandoned the search and jogged off the hill high on adrenaline and retired to Clachaig Inn for a calming dram.

We were badly shaken by how close a call it had been. It was that close to tragedy it's hard to believe we got away with it, and it was one of those events we thought best kept quiet, as it was so nearly a further big tragedy to what sadly lay beneath the deep snow. The media would have had a field day with reporting our near miss, so we just put it behind us. I beat myself up a bit for putting my colleagues at risk as leader out front. Our default position was never to say no and always go look and see if we could get someone out alive. Doing nothing was never an option. Perhaps on this one occasion, it should have been. But then we all knew what mountain rescue involved, and by nature, as mountaineers, we are not risk avoiders. On that occasion the risk couldn't be reduced and nor could the consequences. Three people dying under the snow was a powerful motivator.

Next day and we were back up the hill again. It was hard to probe and hard to dig the debris. The lower corrie was filled in completely and an obvious deep avalanche crown wall was visible under the corrie headwall scarp slope from the initial dry slab avalanche that took out the three casualties. Up above on the west side was another crown from the second wet slab release from when the temperature rose that evening. Possibly the slight thaw and added weight of the sleet and rain were enough to load the snowpack and release it.

It was strange being in such a huge amphitheatre of snow, and also realising what lay deep beneath. And being responsible for the recovery of the missing. The RAF Mountain Rescue Team came and helped us and put in a huge amount of work digging and trenching the impossibly deep snow. Due to the area we were searching being fairly near to the road, fitter TV crews could access the scene, so we were under their watchful eye as well. We put in four days of hard work, shifting tons of snow, but we had to give up and admit defeat, as the snow was too deep. The three walkers remained buried, and the family, especially the wife and mother of two of the casualties, had no closure.

A few days later a massive blizzard struck, main roads were closed, and we got a call in the morning from the police, informing us that three climbers were missing from Curved Ridge on the Buachaille. We parked the yellow rescue trucks we had as mobile base units in the middle of the A82 at the Kingshouse Glen Etive Road Junction as the A82 was closed. Search and Rescue Helicopter call sign Rescue 177 with Adrian "Hands" as pilot landed on the road and John and I had a chat with the crew. I was first on as an observer up front with the pilot and copilot, with Ronnie Rodger in back. We flew around the mountain on what was becoming a post-storm blue sky morning with feet of deep new snow covering everything in sight. Over the radio John Grieve suggested that we fly the east face of the mountain and check out the "Lady's Gully" Central Buttress side. We saw nothing at first. I got "Hands" the pilot to overfly the Chasm, a deep classic summer rock climb with 50m side walls and deep pitches. You could have skied down it that day. The Devil's Cauldron, a feature of the gully, was filled in and an easy snow slope. Snow depth for that must have been about 60 metres (that spring it was fun to climb up the snow chimney and the back wall of the Devil's Cauldron. A cross between caving and rock climbing). Ronnie and I asked to be winched out below Central Buttress, just below "Pontoon", the rock climb, as there appeared to be an avalanche debris pile with new snow on top. We were winched out onto the slope and began to zigzag down.

Soon Ronnie found a glove, then a few feet further down, we found a crampon. We knew we were on the right track for an extended search, and we radioed for the rest of the team to come with shovels and probes. This included Mick Tigh of Lochaber MRT, who was a guide, and who had offered his climbing clients as spot probers. After a couple of hours searching, Tony Sykes, who was on his first year with the rescue team, shouted that he thought maybe he had felt something under his probe. He was very close under the rocks of Central Buttress. The blue sky had gone by this time in the afternoon, and we were again in heavy frontal snow in a blizzard. In about an hour we had dug out the three dead casualties, who were all on top of each other in a tangled mess of ropes and equipment. We excavated them and had stretchers and body bags flown up, and in the blizzard conditions the helicopter crew did a great job. We used a technique used by the Marines in Norwegian winter training to help the aircrew. Very simply, if you have the manpower, you line up folk at intervals both sides of the object to be winched up or landed on to provide a visual reference. As long as the pilot has escape routes on three sides of the approach, they can slowly taxi hover in to the location.

The following day after this body recovery, I was back up at Glencoe to provide ski rescue. On passing the Buachaille, looking across at where the three other folks were still buried, it clicked that at any point in the next weeks or perhaps months, John or I would get a call to look at something poking out of the snow up there. I remember a knot in my stomach and a strange, unhappy feeling.

The wife of the missing father and son came to stay in a bed and breakfast just around the corner from where we lived and was waiting for us to do something when the thaw came. It was to be a very long wait sadly. Knowing she was waiting on resolution was a constant burden for her, and for us. Meanwhile, climbers fell off, got killed and injured, and skiers broke bones as happens in any winter.

The RAF teams came back and had a probe through the avalanche tip over the coming weeks, but nothing was found. Then one day in early April, a walker phoned the police and said he smelled something. John called out the team. We found no smell, but as we were there, we had a probe around, as the level of debris had reduced considerably. We found casualty one a probe length down. An hour later and a bit away, we found number two. During the recovery of number two, something happened inside me. I stayed digging for the next hour until we found and dug out casualty number three at the location where we had been standing the night we were nearly buried ten weeks earlier. After digging him out, I threw down my probe, didn't speak to anyone and walked off the hill. I crossed the bridge at Lagangarbh, where a local undertaker had three grey fibreglass coffins leaning against the fence at the side of the path with the lids off. I glibly remarked that trade had been good from the mountains that winter. Three weeks later I received a £350 donation cheque to the rescue team from him.

I walked past the coffins up onto the road and thumbed a lift to Clachaig where I got very drunk on Scrumpy Jack cider. What Fiona, Esther and Duncan made of the slobbering drunk that arrived home later I have no idea, although I can just recollect Fiona laying me on the couch, taking off my boots and then covering me with a blanket. At some point during the night, I tried to get up the stairs to bed and fell back down, breaking all the pictures lining the staircase on one side as I fell.

I moved on from the above, and I was still very much involved in MR at the front end and dealt with many more horrific events, including people burning in helicopters and finding another two climbing friends (Dougie and Bish Macara) dead. By that time I thought I had better coping mechanisms and I knew about debriefing, and a pint and talking helped. Dealing with traumatic young death diminishes you though. As it should.

In the years to come, folk would say of me at times that I was a driven man. I would drive myself into the ground physically, running, racing my bike or climbing. Although I seemed to cope okay with the extreme stress of life and death decisions, I would get random anxiety attacks over minor things. My local GP sent me to speak to a professional, who over a few months helped me process, until one day a light went on about what my head was telling me. It was shouting at me that I had been feeling like an undertaker in winter, not a medic helping people. Counselling released me from a thinking trap that winter equals death and loss.

The Psychological Cost of Mountain Accidents

Some friends had psychological issues after mountain accidents. Either from direct involvement professionally while guiding, accidents and injury to themselves, or losing friends while mountaineering. My stress and the sequela arising from it was from cumulative events. For others it's a catastrophic single event. Life changing from an accident while climbing or mountaineering. I will tell of one such event affecting a close friend. I have not used names as both persons directly involved are not with us anymore to give permission.

A friend and work colleague at the centre where I was working was taking an advanced winter climbing course candidate out for assessment and asked me to go along as the area and route they wanted to do was Northwest Gully, Stob Coire nam Beith, an area and route I was very familiar with. I knew of some variations to the route that could increase the grade of the climb if needed, while also keeping the exciting finish among that route's spectacular rock scenery. At 1500 feet in length, it is a fine climb, topping out at the summit if you don't mind the easy ground at the end. Stob Coire nam Beith is a big face and has great rock architecture, features such as "The Pyramid" and "The Sphinx" and classic winter routes such as Deep Cut Chimney, which is in the book of classic Scottish winter climbs, *Cold Climbs*. There are also the nice ice pitches of Central Gully Direct via its icefall start. The easiest winter route on the mountain is Summit Gully, a snow climb of 1800 feet, topping out almost at the summit.

That day one of my work colleagues, also a very good friend, had a winter mountaineering training course group with five students. He was going up into the same coire as us. Both our groups met at "The Gate", a place where an old iron gate lies flat next to some iron fence posts in among rock at a flatter part of the coire. We three in our group ate some food and traded some banter, then we got tooled up, ready for the climb above. The other group were going west, below "Hidden Gully" and past a feature known as "The Rognon", a rock island, where they would practise winter skills and then climb out of the coire up the ridge to the summit of the mountain.

Our team of three on the climbing assessment climbed up an icefall into the upper slot of Northwest Gully. Finally, we came out onto the last steep ice pitch at the shoulder, where on an earlier occasion, rescue team member Alan had taken his fall and been injured. Our roped party of three had made good time, and so we decided to traverse east into the Bidean corrie across the top of "Arch Gully", following a way down I knew that takes you into the small high corrie above "Bishop's Buttress". We then descended back down to our van parked at Achnambeithach, and down to the centre for "tea and medals" as we called a brew and cake at the end of a good mountain day. I showered and went home, ready for seeing the kids and hearing of their school day. And hearing from their mum Fiona on how her day had gone. I was barely in the door when the police called on the home phone and asked me to call out the rescue team, as there was a woman badly injured below "Summit Gully", Coire nam Beitheach. I asked for a helicopter and SAR 137 was tasked. I called out the team, then drove up to our arranged meeting point, and with four others, including the instructor I was climbing with earlier, we went back up the mountain laden with vacuum matts, resuscitation kit, casualty bag and a MacInnes Mk7 stretcher. We knew it had to involve the group from the centre we had met up with, as no one else was about that day. No one in the rescue team hangs about, and as members arrived behind us, they radioed me asking me what other gear was needed. I ran through a mental checklist of what we had with us, and what we might also need taken up. It's maybe a 55-minute full gas workout from road to the foot of the gully, going as fast as possible on tired legs.

Our colleague leading the group with the fallen mountaineer met us at the casualty. He had done a very good basic first aid job, turning her on her side to protect her airway, keeping her warm with spare clothing and equipment. She had fallen from near the summit, all the way down to above the Gate where we met earlier. It was a huge fall. Maybe 2000 feet in total length on steep hard snow, including going airborne over a 50ft ice pitch. Her white Petzl helmet was surprisingly only scuffed, but she was not alert and not vocalising, and so it wasn't rocket science medicine to know that her shaken brain would be a mess from traumatic brain injury (TBI). There would also be occult injury, potential spine and chest injury, and perhaps long bone fractures. Despite insulation she was losing heat. This was a potentially fatal triad when hypoxia, loss of blood volume and cold combine. Recue 137 called me for a situation report while he was doing his initial approach into the entrance to the coire. They were flying into the wind and sleet, so it was a big task for them flying in and out safely. We had the casualty on high flow warmed oxygen. We had the stretcher and vacuum mattress ready and warm casualty bag prepared. Sometimes I would go for intravenous access, but on this occasion, there was no time and nothing I could put into a needle would help. In fact the opposite, as it would use up time. Good basic medical care done well is what was needed. Nothing fancy. We worked well as a team. Many of us were used to working, climbing and rescuing with each other. Friends as well as work colleagues. The colleague, the instructor who was with her, was very much involved.

We got her packaged up and secure and ready for uplift. Sometimes I would get lifted up and go into hospital with serious casualties, but that would just be more delay on this occasion, and she didn't need me using up her time. SAR 137 came in at the hover and the world went white in a hurricane of downdraught. We leaned over her to protect her as best we could, the winchman came down, clipped on the stretcher and off up into salvation she went. When SAR 137 backed off and was flying away, I thought just how different the outcome might have been if it couldn't have made it in to lift her. She would die, as her vitals were already bottoming out and she was cold. After the lift came relative quiet, and we got a chance to take stock and care for our mate and his group. He was the ultimate and consummate professional instructor.

As the group were already Winter Mountain Leader trained with an experienced mountaineer among them, this student took on the group leadership to get them back down a safe route of descent, reversing what they had come up earlier. This had allowed the group's instructor to descend Summit Gully to try and find the casualty. He explained what happened to cause the fall. They were on the summit, and she was given a navigation leg to get back down. As it was now clagged in, it was a good learning opportunity. She took a bearing, but the subtle cutback of Summit Gully draws you into it if you go west first. He allowed her to take a few steps until the aspect and slope angle changed and told her to stop and look at the map carefully, which she did, and having established where she was, she realised that she needed to come back up and then go south for a bit first. This is what adventure training in the mountains is all about. Learning in real time in an uncertain and hostile environment. Risk can be managed, not eliminated, and it is learning that can't be done realistically any other way.

It was relatively easy snow terrain, and although very steep below, not overly steep where she turned around. As she turned to come back, she stumbled, perhaps caught a crampon, and fell down into the gully with little opportunity to ice axe arrest and falling into that steepness while gaining speed. Everyone in the group was shocked. It took a great deal of courage for the instructor to descend Summit Gully not knowing what he might find down there, and it's fair to say he was deeply impacted by both a sense of foreboding and responsibility. He conducted himself with a rare courage in such adverse circumstances in my opinion.

She was flown to Belford Hospital, stabilised, then flown down to the specialist head injury unit at the Southern General Hospital. Amongst other things she had a severe traumatic head injury (TBI), and it took years of rehab for her to come back from that. With a TBI folk are seldom the same as before the injury. Remarkably she did recover and went on to marry and have family.

As she was under instruction, there was of course an enquiry to find if lessons could be learned. That was undertaken by a specialist investigation team. Mountains are dangerous, high-risk environments where stuff happens, and we all felt no one was at fault. We have all had accidents and mishaps and difficult things to live with.

Fast forward 16 years from this accident. I received a message from Dave "Heavy" Whalley, ex-RAF MRT legend, now retired, who was still mountaineering and passing on his extensive knowledge. The woman who had fallen had been in contact with him through RAF mountaineering channels and wanted to visit the scene of the accident where she had been injured all those years ago. She wanted to meet me. She had been made aware during the intervening years that the instructor with her that day had lengthy periods of depression, what he and I called "the black dog" as he would speak to me about it. I previously had my own issues from a different accumulation of bad events, but counselling and help from my family got me through it. His stress wasn't the same and manifested very differently, and I think it fair to say it was much more debilitating and harder on his family. He tragically took his life a few years later, having given up mountaineering instructing a couple of years after the event. He was just not happy in the mountains teaching after the accident.

She wanted to talk to me about this, so we met up and chatted about the accident and the aftermath. She was particularly concerned that it had affected the instructor's life and family. Since the accident she had been having regular brain scans, and recently a scan had picked up a brain tumour. Paradoxically perhaps, that terrible fall had saved her life years later. Who knows.

The professional life of a mountaineer can take a heavy toll, as no matter how skilled you are, the risk exposure is many times more than for the amateur. The client base are high achievers, or they wouldn't be with you in the first place, although often folk want the lifestyle and not the risk. Signing up a guide or instructor does not make a remote and hostile environment any less hazardous. The risks can be managed, but only up to a point. A lifetime of serious mountaineering is going to be filled with near misses, and near misses are what give us experience. The sum of these near misses can be a lot of rewarding mountain days, and perhaps some minor A&E time if you're lucky. Or a wooden box six feet under if not. As Edward Whymper, the famous Victorian mountaineer, said after four of his group of seven were killed on the Matterhorn:

"Climb if you will but remember that courage and strength are nought without prudence, and that a momentary negligence may destroy the happiness of a lifetime."

A sad postscript to this tale was to learn that this remarkable and resilient woman who had survived so much had been killed in a motorcycle accident not long after we had met up. Life is cruel beyond words sometimes.

Leaving Mountain Rescue

I left Glencoe MRT after yet another multi-casualty avalanche incident. I had enough, especially as the incident left some questions as to why this particular rescue had not gone well in my view. Fiona felt I had been let down. I had questions and felt lessons could be learned. No one wanted to talk about it. I couldn't understand why.

Fiona said she had supported me for years of married life wondering if I would come back alive from a rescue, and now felt she couldn't do that anymore. So I left MR after 37 years. After leaving, my family at last had a dad that did not run off when a radio went or when a call came from the police asking for the rescue team. Life seemed very relaxed, and we were having fun together as a couple and with our kids.

Sadly, life comes crashing in to remind you not to take anything for granted, and one day 18 months later, Fiona came to the mountain training centre to tell me she had found a small breast lump that morning and had seen the GP. Life changed irrevocably from that moment on. What came next was surgery, chemotherapy and uncertainty. My work's line management were superbly supportive through this first treatment, and I went from full time to a part-time three days a week contract. Everything from then on was about time with my family and not wasting a moment of it. There is no way I could have remained in the rescue team. My family came first. I was so involved with mountain rescue that only an event such as the one mentioned above could cleave me from it. It was providential. Perhaps that's why I feel almost grateful for the way it came about. I remain a firm supporter of the rescue team. A great bunch of folk doing a hard and often very unpleasant and dangerous job. More dangerous than they are willing to admit.

Sadly, even in recent milder winters, there have been some tragic avalanche incidents. Despite milder, wetter winters, there are pulses of extreme weather resulting in very big dumps of snow and high winds. Sometimes these winds come from the east and not the prevailing wind direction, which is normally southwest to northwest. Extreme cold precedes these storms followed by very rapid thawing. This makes weather and avalanche forecasting challenging and travel in mountainous terrain in winter more unpredictable. More uncertainty in an already unpredictable environment.

The emotional toll on rescuers at the avalanche that took a cycling buddy of ours, Chris Bell, hit folk hard. The loss of Danny, a well-known Glencoe skier, in an avalanche off the side of Glencoe Mountain, and the toll of this on his friends and the ski patrollers I work alongside, was considerable. Avalanches cause many of the multi-casualty incidents on the Scottish mountains, and by their very nature and location, they are high-stress events. The quietness at an avalanche, knowing people are asphyxiating, struggling and freezing to death under your feet, that time is life, and that saving that life comes at the end of the shovel you wield is a strange juxtaposition.

"Davy the Bike"

At the time of her diagnosis with stage three breast cancer, Fiona was working as a business manager, running the British Association of Ski Patrollers, who employed out of season ski patrollers to provide first aid training. At that time, the association had grown to employing some full-time as well as part-time first aid trainers. I was one of the part-timers, mainly doing the more advanced medical courses but also the basic first aid training courses, which are a prerequisite for gaining any outdoor instructional award. At this time, the association was training over a thousand folk a year in first aid. Fiona, as an outdoor person, had a unique insight into the outdoor industry and was well respected and well known. Eventually I made the decision to take early retirement from the centre and be at home with her. I thought a small bike business from a big shed in my garden might help bring in some extra money. The bike business was not intended to be anything big. Just a few hire bikes and some spares. For the next nine years I hired out bikes, fixed them and met some wonderful people. I enjoyed just fixing local kids' bikes and if it was simple, it was free. Instead of donating to charity, if a biker was on a sponsored "John O' Groats to Lands' End" cycle ride, I would not charge for time, only spare parts. I built up specialist bespoke road bikes from scratch for some and sorted rust heaps for others. Without really trying I seemed to have a nice, small seasonal business with low overheads. The downside was folk broken down and in distress asking for help at all hours as they were stuck in the middle of nowhere. Or someone who had decided to cycle a hire bike to Oban for the day, then ran out of energy and wanted to get back. Either I went to collect them, or I did not get my bike back. I still seem to have the moniker "Davy the Bike" when folk ask for me, or when I meet folk in a pub.

We were keen cyclists both before and after Fiona's diagnosis. One day we went mountain biking as a family at Learnie Red Rocks on the Black Isle. I jumped a feature on a bike track at about 30mph, coming behind Duncan, who had cleared the jump. I woke up in Raigmore Hospital. My helmet was smashed to smithereens and had been picked up by Helimed and flown to the hospital. The spinal X-ray was clear, but my head was a mess. I had really bad gravel rash, and I also had to have stones which were embedded in my back removed. I possibly had a small skull fracture. After getting out of hospital and on the way home, we stopped for fish and chips at Drumnadrochit where I found I couldn't swallow as my throat had closed up. I had a poor sleep that night, and in the morning I went off to work at the Mountain Training Centre. I felt a slowly progressing numbness up both arms. I asked Henry, one of my work colleagues, to take me to the hospital where one of the consultants whom I knew sorted me out for an urgent MRI scan. Seems I had fluid and bruising around a cervical disc. That still bothers me as any bump to my head causing neck flexion makes my arms go numb and my throat gets sore, although I think that's psychological rather than physical, and it's my mind playing games. I get flashbacks at speed on a mountain bike and this mucks with my head. Briefly waking up fully packaged in a helicopter, staring up at turning rotors, then going back unconscious and later wondering how it's going to play out isn't easy to forget.

The last back injury had probably been a long time coming. Folk talk about having a slipped disc when they have back pain, but let me assure you, a prolapsed disc, if you have one, is amongst the worst possible injuries for pain. Having had a broken ankle, collar bones, fingers and toes, a true slipped (prolapsed) disc was a full ten in the ouch scale for me. For a few years I had warning transient nerve jabs down my legs. I worked hard on my core stability and flexibility to help.

It came to a head after January 1st of that year. While ski patrolling up at Glencoe, I got taken out by a small avalanche that buried me up to my waist and pulled me downhill 50 metres. My bindings didn't release, but I got out of the avalanche tip okay, although humbled. My back definitely took a hit as for the next few days, I couldn't get my socks on without help, and each day started face down on the floor, slowly working up to standing. In my wisdom I decided to do a cross country mountain bike race mid-January. This race involved ducking under and over fallen trees, bog mashing, hitting trees and was general anaerobic hell.

The day after the race, I woke up with my right leg vibrating and having a workout all on its own. Fiona and I went for an easy walk up at the Glencoe Lochan when I noticed I couldn't lift my leg easily. Above Glencoe Lochan my right foot got caught under a tree branch and as I went to step forward, it felt like being shot in the back. Instant pain at level ten, unbearable, and it had me writhing on the ground. After 15 minutes of this Fiona mentioned calling out the rescue team. I wasn't having that, so I got on my feet although I couldn't walk. Freddie Gatting, a friend, was called and came up. Held up between them for support, in an hour or so, they managed to get me down to the car. Passing walkers were all alarmed at the screeching nutter in pain between two women. It was truly excruciating.

Some of the worst pain was inside my kneecaps and joints and felt like hammers were trying to break out, and all the muscles in my right leg were twitching and vibrating. A spine X-ray was inconclusive although it showed a big synovial sack and impingement on my femoral head which might be causing the leg pain. I was referred for a hip MRI, given Tramadol and sent home.

I made the decision to see a good local physiotherapist at Lochaber sports injury clinic and after assessment she concluded my symptoms were definitely from a prolapsed disc. After three of the worst weeks of my life, sleeping curled in a ball and unable to walk, I booked to see a consultant privately at the Nuffield hospital in Glasgow. He saw me two days later, and I was in such a state (some bladder symptoms) that he had the MRI scanner opened up (it was closed for servicing), and I had an MRI. That got looked at and the anaesthetic registrar was called so I could get a second MRI with contrast dye. Within 20 minutes I was looking at my spine in 3D and told by the consultant that if symptoms didn't resolve quickly, I would need surgery.

The consultation was £160, the MRI £350, and I had a diagnosis of an extruded L4/5 with sequestration and left with a DVD of the scan to take to the NHS. An emergency appointment was made by my GP at the Southern General Hospital neurological department. The emergency appointment waiting list time was two months or more! So, what to do? Physiotherapy helped me out with a tailored programme of rehabilitation for my back and hip. My local GP practice was really helpful, and the epilepsy med "Gabapentin" was prescribed. This gave me fantastic dreams, reduced the muscle spasms in my legs and, along with Tramadol and Diclofenac, helped the pain.

I saw the neurosurgeon in May, and he commented that based on the MRI he should operate, but based on seeing me, and that I had been walking, he said that we should hold off as I was doing very well indeed considering how big the extrusion was. I then saw an orthopaedic surgeon and found that I have an impingement in my right femur and a synovial sack, and like most outdoor folk would require a new hip at some point. If I ran, then maybe five years, he said, if I stuck with the bike and skiing, maybe ten. If you X-ray most outdoor folk that I know, they will all be the same from wear and tear from carrying heavy rucksacks. I have bust my ankle on a rescue, bust my collar bones a couple of times on bike crashes, and had quite a few accidents over the years, but that disc prolapse was undoubtedly the most painful, although the neck injury was the scariest and most psychologically damaging.

Loss and Finding My Way

Lance Armstrong, the later discredited cyclist and cancer survivor, was something of an inspiration to us in the early years of Fiona's illness. He authored a book called *It's Not About the Bike*. For us, it was at least partly about the bike, as cycling was a shared activity we both enjoyed.

When able, we were out on our bikes, and eventually mountain biking became a bigger pastime than the road bike. Post-surgery Fiona ripping down the gnarl of the Glen Tress Black Trail was not the activity her surgeon had in mind when recommending keeping fit and taking moderate exercise, but there was no stopping her. I would not dare to try, although tearing myself up wanting to protect her. Meet things head on at full tilt was her way. We had fun getting out maps and following old and sometimes aptly named coffin routes, hill paths that for past generations had been used to carry the dead for burial between Highland communities. We had epic wilderness bike pushes and carries, and also found some wonderful places. Fiona did not ski much by then, but when we did it was mainly exploring over the back Corries at Nevis Range, or a trip to the French Alps, skiing steep stuff with Duncan. She, with her easy-flowing, effortless carving style, me the typical mountaineer skier, working harder, and looking like it too.

I still rescue from the mountains, but on a day shift with Glencoe Ski Patrol mostly, no head torches required. Ski patrol also has its moments of drama with avalanches and injury. I have let my paramedic registration lapse, as I do not feel my clinical skills are sharp, and the yearly training to keep up with development is a toil. I do complete the ski patrol training requirements and annual refreshers when I can, so not all my skills are lost. Aching bones and nagging old injuries require care, and my head is still writing cheques my body struggles to cash. Is that not the case for all adventurous people? Yoga, Ibuprofen, weight training and regular climbing seems to be going fine as long as there are enough rest days in between. Having trained all my life, I am not stopping now. Sport climbing is great fun. Having had injuries to my neck and spine, I am in no hurry to take a ground fall, so clipping bolts and pulling hard suits me.

Some risk aversion has also crept into skiing. After getting avalanched on a ski cut three years ago, my risk appetite is very much reduced. Not completely gone but having reached this far, I do not want the government to keep my old age pension, meagre as it is, because I have written myself off.

I still fly fish although it seems as if I am mostly taking my rod for a walk these days. Casting a fly in a river or loch is a good, mindful way to be in nature. My respect for the fish means I release them all back alive. I fish barbless hooks, and just seeing a fish come at the fly is quite enough. I don't even need to catch them. A few years ago I did Water Bailiff's training via the Institute of Fisheries Management. I did this not so much for poacher prevention but to be able to approach the public and educate them. Of course, removing poachers that are taking what is now a vulnerable species, the Atlantic salmon, is also a part of that. I also recently became a Trustee of the Lochaber Fisheries Trust. I am keen on nature and conservation and support the many initiatives trying to protect our marine habitats and what is in them. In particular the MACOLL group is close to my heart (Marine Area Conservation of Loch Linnhe).

My wonderful family are my blessing, including my grandchild Daisy. Fiona and I were and are so proud of our children's achievements. We never forced education on them, only creating an environment where learning was fun and where we could pass on what skills we had. We supported them in their decisions. That they are all graduates is down to their hard work at sticking with it. We would never have judged had they decided university was not for them. I often find it ironic that at interviews much of what enhances their employability are the skills like climbing, skiing and gardening we passed on, and their willingness to work in a variety of summer hospitality jobs when young. These carry weight with prospective employers. Most of the soft skills come from their mother. The ability to articulate words perhaps from me, as I am the wordy one. Esther, my daughter, and her partner Ryan with wee Daisy live in Strathaven, a lovely little town. Duncan, my son, is back in the UK with Hannah, his wife, after going to Australia to work on a South Australian Covid project. Rebekah, my youngest, is settled with Connor in Edinburgh. Fiona would be so proud of them.

I miss and mourn Fiona, who was part of my life for 45 good years. She was not one for self-pity and would be the first to tell me to get off my backside and live. So that is what I will try to do. And this living still includes a wee bit of risk. Risk of the heart and of the soul too. For a while I was like someone perched on a rock in the middle of the River Coe, not able to leave one bank and the past, able to step to another, the future. Now I have made that step across. Good memories remain, and there are some new ones to make with friends and very special people.

It is said that before entering the sea
a river trembles with fear.
She looks back at the path she has travelled,
from the peaks of the mountains,
the long winding road crossing forests and villages.
And in front of her,
she sees an ocean so vast,
that to enter
there seems nothing more than to disappear forever.
But there is no other way.
The river cannot go back.
Nobody can go back.
To go back is impossible in existence.
The river needs to take the risk
of entering the ocean
because only then will fear disappear,
because that is where the river will know
it is not about disappearing into the ocean,
but of becoming the ocean.

– Kahlil Gibran